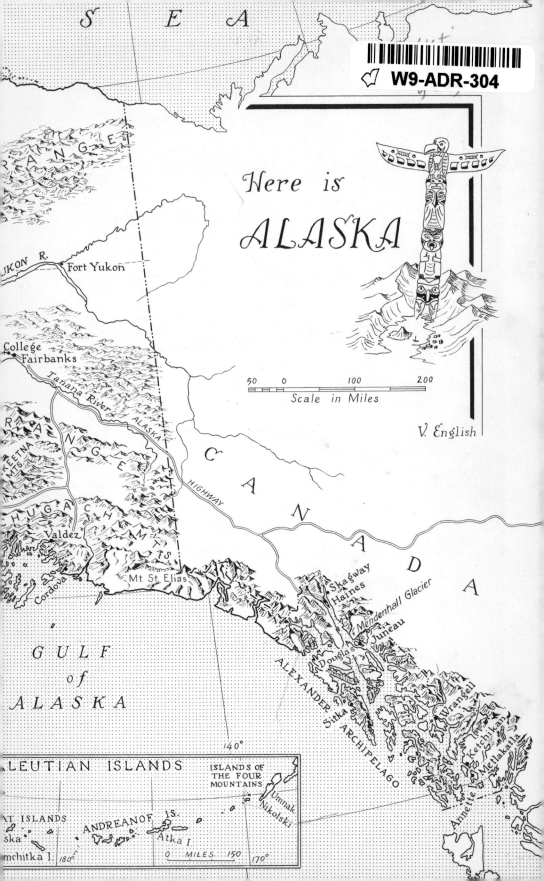

S E A

R A N G E

YUKON R. • Fort Yukon

Here is
ALASKA

College
Fairbanks

Tanana River

50   0   100   200

Scale in Miles

V. English

RANGE

ALASKA

C A N A D A

TALKEETNA MTS

CHUGACH MTS

HIGHWAY

Valdez

Cordova

Mt. St. Elias

Skagway
Haines

Mendenhall Glacier

Juneau
Douglas

GULF

of

ALASKA

ALEXANDER

Sitka

Nikolski

ARCHIPELAGO

Wrangell

Ketchikan

Metlakatla

Annette I.

140°

ALEUTIAN ISLANDS

ISLANDS OF
THE FOUR
MOUNTAINS

Umnak

FAT ISLANDS

ANDREANOF IS.

ska

mchitka I. 180°

Atka I.

0   MILES   150   170°

HERE IS ALASKA

EVELYN STEFANSSON

HERE IS

ALASKA

REVISED STATEHOOD EDITION

CHARLES SCRIBNER'S SONS   NEW YORK

✖ *Acknowledgements* ✖

The author wishes to express her special appreciation to former bush
pilot Raymond Petersen, now President of *Northern Consolidated
Airlines* in Anchorage, who made her Alaskan journey possible.

GRATEFUL ACKNOWLEDGMENT IS MADE FOR PERMISSION TO USE
THE FOLLOWING:

Photograph on page 39 courtesy of *Alaska Airlines*

Photographs on pages 40, 160-161 courtesy of *Alaska Coastal Airways*

Photograph on page 37 from *Alaska Visitors Association*

Photographs on pages 112, 150 from *American Museum of Natural
History*, New York

Photographs on pages 126, 129, 132-133 by *Ted Bank II* from *Monk-
meyer*

Photograph on page 35 from *Coon Bros.*, Sitka

Map on pages 86-87 and endpapers by *Van English*

Photographs on pages 168, 169 from *General Dynamics Corp.*

Photograph on page 67 by *Richard Harrington*

Photographs on pages 2, 147 by *Victor Heusser*, courtesy of *Geophysical
Institute, University of Alaska*

Photograph on page 61 (bottom) from *Lomen Bros.*, Nome

Photographs on title page and pages 5, 9, 30-31, 46, 50, 58-59, 62,
65, 68, 70, 73, 77, 83, 84, 91, 95, 100-101, 102-103, 104, 105,
108-109, 138, 139, 152-153, 156-157, 158 by *Frederick Machetanz*

Schematic drawing on page 57 courtesy of *Smithsonian Institution*

Photographs on page 61 (top) from *National Museum*, Copenhagen

Photographs on pages 14-15, 17, 27, 42-43, 45, 55 from *Pan American
World Airways*

Photograph on pages 144-145 courtesy of *University of Alaska*

Photographs on pages 6-7, 22-23, 24 by *Western Electric*

The photographs on the following pages were taken by the author,
Evelyn Stefansson; Pages 10, 11, 12, 26, 89, 93, 106, 116, 118,
121, 140, 146, 162, 164, 165

For Mary *and* Anne

NOTE

Alaska's flag, "eight stars of gold on a field of blue" forming the Big Dipper and the great North Star, was designed by a thirteen-year-old Indian boy. Benny Benson, a seventh grade pupil at the Mission Territorial School at Seward, won first prize in the Alaska Flag Contest. His simple, handsome design was officially adopted by the Territorial Legislature in 1927.

✂ *Foreword* ✂

To an extent this volume is a by-product of research done in New York City from 1932 to 1945 for Pan American World Airways, and from 1936 to 1951 for the Army, Navy and Air Forces of the United States. Through rather unusual circumstances the book, originally planned by the publishers with another author, came to be written by a member of our research staff.

An important part of our northern research always has been correspondence with men who live in places like Alaska, Arctic Canada, Lapland and Siberia. One of our valuable Alaska correspondents was Frederick Machetanz.

Around 1940 Machetanz was in New York planning with his publishers a third book on Alaska, when he was called up for active service in World War II. In his predicament and theirs, the publishers and he asked me to do the text for which Fred had already accumulated most of the illustrations. But I was preoccupied with war work also, as adviser to various Government departments; so, by mutual agreement, HERE IS ALASKA was undertaken by one of our researchers who, among others, was concerned with Alaska and other northern Sailing Directions, under a contract we had with the Hydrographic Office of our Navy.

As with the Sailing Directions, HERE IS ALASKA was to Evelyn a research job through which, with some advice from me, she successfully implemented, and to an extent modified, the plans that were given her to start from. That was in 1942 and 1943. The book did well, and continued selling steadily; but Alaska ceased being a Territory, became our largest State, and there was much other change.

Meantime Evelyn, in addition to publishing two more volumes, had seen many arctic countries she had previously known from books, pictures and hearsay. On only one of her journeys she reached Alaska from the North, by one of the early Scandinavian Airlines flights from Copenhagen. In Alaska she took a Northern Consolidated Airways flying job to visit intimately and widely the Territory, as it then still was, and in order to take her own photographs. She studied and lectured at the University of Alaska. Here at Dartmouth she has played, before and since, a role in our Arctic Seminar, and is consulted by students and faculty on northern matters.

Hence, and for other reasons, this rewriting and republishing of HERE IS ALASKA.

Vilhjalmur Stefansson, *Arctic Consultant*
Dartmouth College
NORTHERN STUDIES PROGRAM
Hanover, New Hampshire

⊱ Contents ⊰

List of Illustrations

>< *HERE IS ALASKA* ><

The Aurora Borealis paints Alaska's northern skies with light and color.

≍ *Chapter One* ≍

Forty=Ninth State

On the night of June 30, 1958, the United States Senate, by a vote of 64 to 20, touched off a gigantic celebration that extended from Alaska's mild, wooded, southeastern shores to its northernmost permafrosted tip, Point Barrow. Huge bonfires had been prepared, and the moment word was received they were kindled by jubilant crowds. Bands, speeches, fireworks, parades, shouting and dancing in the streets were all part of joyous demonstrations that lasted through the night and well into the day. For the bill the Senate had passed at 8:02 P.M. assured the admission of the Territory of Alaska into the Union as our forty-ninth state. On August 26th, in the heaviest election turn-out in Alaska's history, her people voted five to one in favor of statehood.

Alaska was ready for this moment! Three years before she had adopted the Tennessee Plan, a program drawn up and first applied in 1796 by the vigorous pioneers of the Territory of Tennessee in *their* fight for statehood. The first item called for by the Plan was a constitutional convention. In September, 1955, therefore, Alaska's Territorial Legislature elected fifty-five convention delegates, and the following November all of them gathered on the campus of the University of Alaska. Here in the handsome, brand-new Student Union building, a seventy-five day session began, during which a constitution was drafted. Political scientists pronounced it a "model" and Alaskans agreed, for when it was submitted to them for approval they adopted it by a vote of more than two to one.

Continuing the Tennessee Plan, the convention provided for the immediate election of two "senators" and a "representative" from Alaska to go to Washington. These phantom legislators, who of course had no legal status in Congress, were charged with going simply to lobby for Alaskan Statehood. Former Governor Ernest Gruening was one senator-elect, William A. Egan, of Valdez, president of the constitutional convention, the other. Ralph J. Rivers was the lone representative. Go to Washington they did, in a blaze of newspaper headlines and of numerous radio and television interviews. Combining forces with Alaska's beloved delegate, E. L. Bartlett, these well-informed, able men brought the attention of Washington and the nation to reasons why Alaska should become a state. In the time between his governorship and his "senatorship," Gruening had written a penetrating political history of the Territory, called *The State of Alaska,* setting forth past misgovernment, present problems, and the arguments favoring statehood. Young Mike Stepovich, the first Alaska-born governor ever appointed to that office, had also helped the fight; so too had the Secretary of the Interior, Fred Seaton, the first man in his position to interest himself deeply in Alaska and her problems. Now at last their efforts were successful.

To the majority of Alaskans, alerted and tense, word of statehood arriving by radio and telephone brought news of victory—a battle won. Statehood isn't something that happens

The first newspapers announcing statehood.

automatically to a Territory. Alaskans from all walks of life had labored hard and long to achieve it. To them it meant an end of colonialism. It meant an end to "taxation-without-representation." In the past, while Delegate Bartlett might make speeches in the halls of Congress, he had no vote, despite the payment of Federal income taxes by his constituents. It meant at last the possibility of controlling the one-way traffic in the largely absentee-owned fishing and mining industries. For almost since the purchase of Alaska in 1867, these industries had drained her riches. Money, equipment, even some labor, came from outside and profits went outside, leaving Alaska depleted and empty-handed. But perhaps the most important reaction to statehood for Alaskans was a happy feeling of equality with all other United States citizens—a coming-of-age.

Now at last they could be masters of their own destiny instead of the victims of distant exploiters and frequently uninformed though sometimes kindly Washington legislators.

The safety of Alaska's outermost coasts, some of them within sight of Siberia, is now insured. A large portion of the rich dowry she brings to her union with the United States is her strategic position. On the north Alaska faces the Arctic Sea, newest aerial crossroads of the world; to the west across Bering Sea and Strait lies the Soviet Union. Two huge, costly defense alarm systems now guard these shores. One is the DEW Line, or Distant Early Warning radar screen, which starts in the Canadian Arctic and girdles the North American mainland west-

From the air, a typical DEW Line station cluster of buildings and equipment surrounding the dome-shaped housing of the main search antenna.

ward to Alaska. Here it continues along her northern and western shores to and through the Aleutian Islands. The second defense installation is White Alice, a complicated communications system using huge twin antennas, sixty feet high, set up at stations about two hundred miles apart. However bothersome the sun spots or stormy the weather, whatever the hour of day or night, White Alice provides certain communication between outposts and mainland in an area where radio blackouts occur at unexpected intervals and may last a fortnight. Now White Alice, the latest in tropospheric electronics, stands guard from villages where Eskimos still hunt whales from skin-covered umiaks.

Statehood will not solve all of Alaska's problems. Indeed, in the process of solving some, new ones will be created. There is bound to be an interim period of uncertainty and change that may be difficult and even hurtful to some of her people. But although growing up is often a painful experience for an individual, grow up he must or warp his personality. So it is with youthful Alaska, who certainly gives every indication of growing in all sorts of ways.

Since 1940 her population has more than doubled. Anchorage and Fairbanks are booming cities, complete with modern housing developments, motels, parking meters, and traffic problems. Her incredibly rich resources are being developed, some of them for the first time. Fishing and mining, long the most important industries, and still important, have been overtaken by the defense industry, with pulp manufacturing and petroleum, both new to Alaska, showing great promise. The recent discovery of Alaska's first rich commercial oil fields just outside Anchorage started an oil-leasing rush reminiscent of early Klondike days.

But that rush, however, is an exception to today's rule. The get-rich-quick adventurers, who first stormed Alaska's ports in Gold Rush days, have been followed by more serious-minded citizens. These young people, and most of them *are* young, are not primarily interested in making a rich strike and hurrying "outside" to spend it. They seem to care most about new and better schools for their children, improved housing and economic conditions, and encouraging cultural activities such as Anchorage's music festival which brings a host of famous soloists to Alaska each year. With the exception of the military population (which in 1958 was about 40,000), today's typical resident is a permanent settler who intends to grow up with the new state.

Forty-Ninth State

Our newest state is our largest state. Indeed, Alaska is two and a quarter times the size of Texas. Her area, 586,400 square miles, increases the total square mileage of the United States to more than three and a half million. Her numerous islands and indented shores add more than 33,000 miles to our coastlines. Her soils and mountains contain thirty-one of the thirty-three so-called strategic minerals, in addition to proven deposits of natural gas, rich oil lands, and possibilities of almost infinite hydroelectric power. California's Mount Whitney must now hand over the title of "tallest mountain in the States" to Alaska's 20,320-foot Mount McKinley, already bearer of an old title "highest in North America." Alaska is our only state which extends into the Eastern Hemisphere, for the Aleutian Islands reach beyond the 180th meridian to about 172° east longitude. This is a big, tall, wide, rich record-breaking new state!

Petersburg's harbor is crowded with some of the boats that make and keep the fishing industry important.

Gold is still mined, largely by huge dredges. Here we see a portion of one, a continous bucket belt which scoops up ore below the water line carrying it to the heart of the dredge where it is separated.

For so vast an area, Alaska has relatively few inhabitants. Indeed, she displaces Nevada, the state which formerly had fewest people. But though she lacks numbers, Alaska's population is younger and more energetic than that of other states. The average Alaskan is only twenty-six years old, five years younger than the average in the rest of the United States. This youthfulness is responsible for Alaska having the highest birth rate and lowest death rate of any state. In 1958 her civilian population numbered about 170,000, of which almost one fifth, about 35,000, were Eskimos, Aleuts, and forest Indians. Two of these peoples, the Eskimo and the Aleut, we need to know better than we do. Each may be thought of as a kind of Indian, indeed, some anthropologists speak of "Eskimo Indians" and "Aleut Indians." Although once far more numerous than they are today, Alaska's natives are now faring better than in recent decades. For one thing, they are *surviving*. At long last, their birth rate exceeds their death rate. Among all peoples whose ancestors were never exposed to the disease, tuberculosis is one of the greatest killers. Soon after the white man's coming to Alaska, it began to claim Eskimo and Indian lives; and it continued to do so in terrifying numbers. Now at last the disease has been curbed, if not stopped, and the outlook for control is bright, thanks to a vigorous United States Public Health Service Program and the co-operative Alaska Health Department.

The two things Alaska needs most to assure and secure a prosperous future are settlers and investment capital. She needs the capital in order to produce cement from her limestone, lumber and paper from her forests, refined fuels from her oil reserves, and food from her fertile lands. Her rich resources can easily support the greatly expanded population required to make this dream come true and reward the necessary labor and capital.

Statehood brings the dream closer.

In summertime Juneauites may swim in surroundings of incomparable beauty.

Chapter Two

Fact and Fable

Alaska is a land of extremes—of the very old and the very new, of ancient Eskimo and Indian cultures and modern pulp mills and fisheries. Here you will find, side by side, glaciers and strawberries, dog teams and airplanes. A skin boat, the design of which has not changed for a thousand years, is fitted with the latest model outboard motor.

The state of Alaska offers almost every conceivable type of climate and country. Between southeastern Alaska and the northernmost arctic slope are magnificent snow-clad mountains, vast forests, broad prairies. Alaska has the third largest river in North America, the Yukon, placed by its length and drainage basin after the Mississippi and Mackenzie. It has innumerable small lakes, no large ones.

One of the commonest mistakes made about Alaska is that it is a frigid country, so chilled that there are no summers. But two-thirds of Alaska lies below the Arctic Circle, and even at Point Barrow, its north tip, the lowest winter temperature is slightly above the lowest records of North Dakota, Wyoming, and Montana. In central Alaska the maximum heat of summer is about equal to that of New York City.

The persistent myth that it never gets warm in Alaska was exploded many years ago by explorers and travelers. The U. S. Weather Bureau has recorded temperatures of 100° F. in the shade at Fort Yukon, just north of the Arctic Circle, 99° at Fairbanks, just south of the Circle, and similar highs for other places. Compare these with the highest recorded temperature of Palm Beach, Florida, which is about 96°.

Many Alaska travelers who have been in the tropics say they have suffered from heat in the Arctic and from cold in the tropics. This is not as strange as it sounds. The heat in the Arctic is usually humid. In summer, the days grow longer and longer until, for a short period, they are twenty-four hours long, and the sun never sets. The heat is continuous; there is no cooling-off period. In the tropics, the air has a chance to

cool during the long nights and does not start heating up again until the sun comes out next day. While the summer season is shorter in the Arctic than in the tropics, without the relief of cool nights it may feel harder to endure.

To most people who have heard about how cold it is up north, the summer heat comes as a surprise. And the mosquitoes! Unless you have been in the north in summertime, it is hard to visualize and impossible to describe the terrific number of mosquitoes that exist. Formerly, no European traveler dared move into the bush country, or out upon the prairies, without a headnet, gloves, and heavy clothing lashed tightly at wrist and ankle to protect him against the pests. Thanks to the invention during World War II of several fairly effective mosquito repellents, he can now wear lighter clothing without being at the mercy of biting insects.

Some of Alaska's biggest and best trout come from the Russian River on the Kenai Peninsula.

Mosquitoes do not breed as well in a lake as in a swamp; they need many small puddles of water. In most of the Yukon Valley, when you dig below the surface a few inches, the ground is permanently frozen. Last winter's snow water and yesterday's rain cannot penetrate downward through the hard-as-concrete frost but stays on the surface to form innumerable swamps, each an ideal breeding place for mosquitoes.

Eternally frozen subsoil, or permafrost, as it is now called, underlies the northern two-thirds of Alaska. Experts tell us it occurs beneath one-fifth of the entire earth's land surface. Half of Canada and much of the northern Soviet Union have permafrost. Wherever it occurs, lack of underground drainage results in thousands, or, more likely, millions of lakes, ranging in size from small puddles to many square miles. When you fly over permafrost country it has a typical look—half or even more of the ground below is covered by innumerable lakes of all sizes and shapes. These lakes provide good landing places for pontoon planes in summer and wheel- or ski-equipped aircraft in winter. Permafrost lakes form only on rolling or level ground, of course.

Alaskans probably fly more than any other people in the world. There is one plane for every 150 people in Alaska, seventeen times the average of her sister states. If Alaskans have any rivals in this respect, they will be found in other northern countries where huge areas are spanned by few railroads or automobile roads, and where ice conditions limit the shipping season to a short summer period.

Horseshoe Lake in Mt. McKinley National Park is typical of the grandeur and beauty of the state.

Along the suburban lake shores of Anchorage you will see rows of neatly moored pontoon planes awaiting their owner-pilots. Most are small craft which take off or land on any of Alaska's numberless lakes. Families living in Alaska's largest city use them to "get away from the congestion of city life." They bring spare parts, machinery, mail, fresh food, and relief workmen to remote mining and oil developments. They pick up and deliver trappers, fishermen, scientists, tourists, or weekend campers. They taxi doctors, nurses, and patients in and out of the bush and permit a minister to visit the farthest borders of his parish. Nowadays much preliminary prospecting for metals and oil is done from the air; so is mapping, in a fraction of the time formerly required. Almost a thousand children go to school by plane in Alaska, salesmen visit their customers and some prosperous Eskimo women at Point Barrow are said to fly south regularly to Fairbanks, a thousand-mile round trip, to have their hair done.

In tiny, distant villages, the bush pilot plays an important role. Usually one man does all the flying to and from a small village. He knows the terrain by heart and has made friends with the local weather. He will fly in weather other flyers would not dare attempt. He is a combination mailman, ambulance driver, personal shopper, and Santa Claus. Sometimes he is the only link between the village and the outside world. Of necessity he is their confidant; he is their newsbearer, and usually is adored by the villagers. If he has any unusual personality traits they are discussed with relish and woven into a kind of folklore that follows him for the rest of his life.

Alaska has, in 1958, twice as many miles of civil airways as roadways, and airport construction continues at an astounding pace. Since 1956, transpolar flights from Europe to Asia across the Arctic Sea stop at Anchorage to refuel. Now Alaskans who wish to go to Europe no longer need fly by way of Seattle and New York. They may board a plane at Anchorage and fly directly by the shortest route via the North Pole, saving thousands of miles, many hours, and considerable fare.

There are two railroads in all of Alaska; the Alaska Railroad, whose main line operates from Seward to Fairbanks, and the White Pass and Yukon, which runs through only twenty miles of Alaska on its way from Skagway to Whitehorse, in Canada's Yukon Territory. The Alaska Railroad is government-operated and has 470 miles of main stem. In summertime the daylight trip, about twelve hours from Fairbanks to Anchorage, is a favorite with tourists, for it cuts through the heart of Alaska, with magnificent scenery all the way. Not long ago, with the acquisition of modern sleeping cars, overnight service was inaugurated during the winter months, when daylight service is suspended.

One of the Railroad's more unusual problems is keeping moose off the tracks. The moose death toll in 1956 was 250. Special cattle guards have been installed on the engine cars with a hope of diminishing the casualties.

One of the most popular stops on the Alaska Railroad is at Mount McKinley National Park, where the chief attraction is the mighty mountain the Indians call *Denali,* meaning "home of the sun." Mount McKinley is one of the most dramatic sights in a land which abounds in stunning scenery. The light tan granite mass, crown of the Alaska Range, climbs upward to a height of 20,320 feet, almost four miles! No other mountain in the world rises so far above its own base. The upper two-thirds of the peak is permanently snow-covered, and often takes on a pinkish glow at sunrise and sunset.

McKinley Park is the farthest north and second-largest United States national park. It was created by an Act of Congress in February, 1917, and covers over three thousand square miles. Its snow-capped peaks and grinding glaciers slope down into spruce-forested valleys. The park abounds in wild life. Caribou, giant Alaska moose, handsome white Dall mountain sheep, and grizzly bear are some of the animals which might be seen by a lucky tourist from a train window as the railroad speeds through the park.

When the Alaska Road Commission was formed back in 1905, there were less than a dozen miles of passable wagon road in Alaska. Today the picture is very different. The famous Alaska Highway connects Canada with Alaska. This road, almost fifteen hundred miles long, was completed during a wartime emergency in November, 1942, thanks to the almost superhuman efforts of both Canadian and American military and civilian construction men. As soon as it was finished, in a record-breaking eight months, military equipment began streaming in from the States through Canadian Edmonton and Whitehorse, to Fairbanks, the Alaskan terminus. After the war, tourists followed, in growing numbers each year.

In 1948, spurred by a tense world political situation, the United States military personnel examined Alaska again. Her geographical position gave her new value in an atomic and hydrogen age. Facing the Arctic Sea on the north, almost touching Siberia on the west, and bounding the North Pacific to the south, Alaska stood virtually undefended. Huge military installations were built. As they were completed, they demanded new and improved roads.

The highway system of 1958 includes a thousand-mile network of all-weather paved roads. They connect the ice-free ports of Valdez, Seward, and Haines with interior Alaska's principal cities and military installations, as well as with the other forty-eight states. A secondary system of 2,594 miles connects farming, mining, and industrial areas to the main network. Lastly, 570 miles of isolated road connects settled places with air, rail, or water transportation facilities.

In recent years, as the speed and range of airplanes increased, so did our understanding of great circle air routes. The Arctic or Polar Sea, surrounded by the world's most powerful nations, assumed a new and to some, ominous, importance. The shape of our earth was re-examined in the light of long range missiles and jet planes. The old east-west air routes have become as dated as biplanes. The new routes lead north or cross the arctic regions slantingly. If hostile planes ever approach our land, we believe they will come, not from the Atlantic or Pacific, but from beyond the North Pole. All possible warning will be needed to ready our defenses.

In response to this need, in 1952, the Distant Early Warning Line of radar stations was created. Known more familiarly as the DEW Line, the function of its numerous outposts, ringing northern Canada and Alaska, is to warn us of the approach of enemy planes. To test the feasibility of the idea and to solve some of the new problems dealing with large scale construction in a strange land, a sample station, a kind of guinea pig outpost, was constructed. Completed successfully, it was followed with greater speed by the largest assault upon the Arctic (in terms of men, ships, materials and equipment) in the entire history of the Northland.

Every known means of transportation was utilized, and a few new ones invented. By ship, by plane, by long tractor-driven sledge trains, by river barge and by giant new rubber-wheeled vehicles that could travel over snowy roadless tundra in summer and winter, all converged in the course of a single year on North America's northernmost continental shore. Hampered by the need for developing special methods to deal with short summers, ice-choked waterways, permafrost, muskeg, (a thick, spongy water-logged carpet of mosses and sedges) cold temperatures, and humid summer heat, the engineers pushed on. The successful completion of the DEW Line in a sur-

prisingly short time was a victory over stupendous obstacles—
one of the most challenging assignments ever undertaken in
the Arctic.

A hazard associated with life in the Far North is
the uncertainty of radio reception. Radios have a way of
suddenly going dead, abruptly cutting off the only means of
communication between distant outposts. Sometimes, too, sudden noisy atmospheric static will blot out the signal. Since such
interruptions might prove disastrous in time of war, the Defense Department, as part of our continental defense and the

general fortification of Alaska, built a huge communications network designed to keep us in touch with our farthest Alaskan outposts, whatever the weather. The code name of the project, while secret, was White Alice, and it still bears the name.

On November 30, 1956, the first link of White Alice's chain of thirty-nine stations was finished. Each station is equipped to both receive and transmit signals, using a new and advanced method of radio relay, never before used on such a large scale. Good telephone and telegraphic communications are

The modern pattern formed by a DEW Line station has become a familiar sight on our northernmost shores.

maintained between stations, whether skies are stormy or clear. Huge scoop-shaped, sixty-foot-high antennas, each weighing one hundred tons, are used to beam signals into the troposphere, the five-mile layer of air that extends upward from the earth. In the troposphere the signals are "scattered" and only a tiny fraction of the energy sent out arrives at the receiving antenna. Here it is amplified until intelligible. Identical antennas, spaced at distances of up to two hundred miles, receive the signals and retransmit them if necessary. In a country where few roads and extreme conditions make ordinary wire circuits difficult and expensive to maintain, this is an ideal system.

While White Alice was designed primarily to enable the Air

The route of White Alice Communications network. Western Electric was prime contractor for construction of the network.

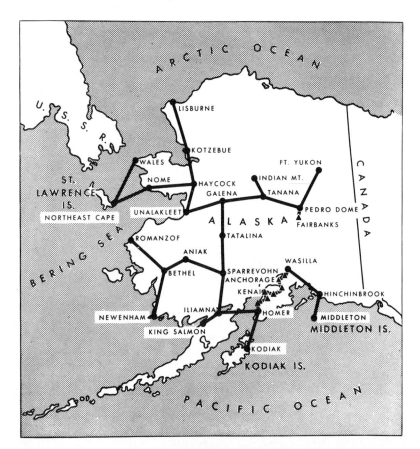

White Alice provides another new landscape for Alaska. This station in the Matanuska Valley has twin 60-foot antennas and a horn antenna atop a 175-foot tower.

Forces to keep in touch with radar outposts, all government departments, civilian telephone and telegraph agencies, as well as the people of Alaska, will benefit in peacetime from the $140,000,000 system.

Many White Alice stations are built on high mountain tops, where radio conditions are usually best. The distinctive twin-antennas, resembling outdoor movie screens, except that they are curved rather than flat, now bring reliable telephone service to communities and remote settlements that never had it before.

For centuries Alaska's rivers were her only highways.

For centuries Alaska's principal interior highways were her rivers. In summer they served as liquid avenues for Eskimo kayak and umiak and Indian canoe. Later the white man introduced paddle-wheeled, wood-burning steamboats, and other craft. After fall freeze-up, rivers are transformed into broad ice highways on which dog teams, horse teams, or tracked vehicles travel. More and more freighting is being done throughout the North by caterpillar tractors, or "cats" as they are called, pulling long trains of heavily loaded freight sledges. In building the DEW Line, a new kind of vehicle was introduced. This was a huge houselike truck, with giant rubber-tired wheels, taller than a man, which rolled effortlessly across the roadless, snow-covered frozen muskeg. Teams of drivers ate and slept in them and took turns driving. They traveled in fleets for safety, helping each other in case of engine trouble or other emergencies.

Every tiny village in Alaska, even a lone wilderness camp, has a short-wave radio receiving and sending set. The two-way radio is vital for survival in many parts of Alaska, especially the sparsely settled areas. It combines the virtues of newspaper, telephone, telegraph, and a visit across the back fence with a neighbor. It is the link with civilization, the source of help in troubled times, the bearer of tidings, good and bad. If a plane is overdue, you first hear of it on the radio. If a listener has news of it, he reports. If hours go by without word, rescue plans take form and are put into action.

Sternwheelers on the Yukon River were once a familiar sight.

Sometimes homey messages are heard through the innumerable privately owned two-way radios, reminders for someone to bring home a pound of hamburger and a dozen eggs from town. Recipes and gossip are exchanged. Chess games are played, a move or two a day, by players hundreds of miles apart. Strangers in the area are sure to be mentioned, their business and personalities discussed, and usually unbeknownst to them, their movements will be followed with friendly interest.

The short-wave radio dispenses medical information to isolated villages, especially in emergencies, where a plane would be unlikely to arrive in time, or when weather prevents the flight. Operations have been performed by schoolteachers and others with little or no knowledge of surgery, step by step, according to instructions from a doctor who may be a thousand miles away and who calmly, quietly asks questions and gives directions. Countless babies have been delivered by this unusual hospital of the air waves.

Weather reports, by which the aviator lives, are broadcast at regular intervals and by request. Nowhere in the world, I believe, is there so much talk of weather as in Alaska. Good weather means flights on time, mail, groceries, machinery, and people delivered on schedule. Bad weather means waiting and more waiting, no mail, no flights, boredom, frustration, standstill. Where the plane is one's only link with "outside," talk about cold fronts, cloud ceilings, fog, moon, and visibility is pertinent talk.

In dollars, fishing is still the largest commercial enterprise in Alaska, and the huge salmon take still far outstrips all other types of fish. For the single year of 1956 canned salmon alone was valued at $76,919,415.00. Herring and halibut are also caught, and more recently shellfish. The enormous and delicious king crab is becoming famous outside as well as throughout Alaska.

But if you ask an Alaskan to name the most important industry he is likely to answer, "Defense." More than $100,000,000 was spent, in 1956 alone, building airfields, bases, radar and communications lines. This has created employment for thousands of Alaskans and brought outside specialists to the land. In some areas it has created a "boom" atmosphere that worries a few who think ahead to the times when it may stop.

The pulp industry, non-existent a decade ago, now exports its product from a huge new mill at Ketchikan. Another, only slightly smaller, at Sitka, built with Japanese capital, is scheduled for completion in 1960. Other pulp mills in the Panhandle, as the narrow southeastern strip of Alaska is called, are in the development stage.

A brand-new and fast-increasing boost to Alaska's economy — is the tourist trade. Each year in greater numbers, travelers flock to the state by car, along the Alaska Highway, by leisurely boat through the Inside Passage, but most of all by air. Thanks to excellent connections, a Texan or a New Yorker, with a two-week vacation, can travel north of the Arctic Circle, view the midnight sun, photograph totem poles or the tallest mountain in North America, or set foot on a startlingly beautiful glacier in southern Alaska. He can visit Indian and Eskimo villages, talk with their inhabitants and watch them perform ancient dances. For that indispensable ritual, part of every holiday to a far place, he can purchase innumerable fascinating native handicrafts to take home for souvenirs.

Mining, once the foremost industry of Alaska, is now only third in importance, gold production, its mainstay, having greatly declined. Today coal, gold, and a "new" mineral, sand and gravel for road and airfield building, are mined in about equal values. Uranium production started in 1957. Nineteen oil companies were actively prospecting when the first rich commercial strike was made in 1957. Farming is becoming an industry to reckon with, especially in the fertile Matanuska and Tanana valleys. But fur production and fur farming, once sizable, have faded to ghosts of their former importance.

The colorful whaling industry used to be important in Alaska and was revived after the Civil War. The two chief uses for whalebone then were to stiffen women's corsets and to make

At Point Hope whales are still hunted by the Eskimos for food. Here they have harpooned one.

buggy whips. Tailors used it too for making men's shoulders appear broader and squarer than they actually were.

In summer whaling ships used to sail through Bering Strait and east along the north coast of Alaska. The first vessels wintered in 1889 at Herschel Island, just west of the Mackenzie

River delta, in what was supposed to be U. S. territory but was later determined to be Canadian. Many whales were captured north of Bering Sea and the Alaskan mainland.

Ships used to winter two or three times on a voyage. The crew usually numbered forty-nine because law required any ship carrying fifty or more men to have a doctor aboard, and the owners were canny to avoid this expense. The largest whales gave two thousand pounds of bone, which, at four dollars per pound, netted eight thousand dollars. The record catch on a single voyage was sixty-nine whales, the average perhaps one thousand pounds of bone. The profits were impressive for some but not for the men before the mast. They worked for a percentage, sometimes as low as 1/200th share, and easily managed to spend their earnings on what the skipper sold them from the slop chest. These percentages were called lays. Those of the crew members were very small; the captain's very large, sometimes enabling him eventually to buy his own ship, and the lion's share went to the owners.

This romantic and, for the owner, lucrative business came to a sudden close around 1906. That year more than a dozen ships had wintered at Herschel Island, or points east; thereafter no more than two or three ships wintered, and these devoted themselves almost wholly to trading.

The failure of the whalebone industry was caused by three things which happened together. Women stopped wearing heavily-boned corsets, men stopped using buggy whips because the automobile was coming in, and somebody invented a substitute called featherbone. Whalebone dropped in price from four or five dollars per pound to fifteen or twenty cents, and, indeed was difficult to sell at any price except in very small quantities.

While commercial whaling died out in Alaska, Eskimo whaling continued, as it had for centuries before the white men took it up. Commercial whalers usually had taken only the whalebone, or black baleen, wastefully discarding the rest of the huge mammals. But to the Eskimo, the whale is food, and one or two whales caught per season spell the difference for an entire village between a year of plenty and a year of want. They love its nourishing meat, and consider the skin, with an inch-thick layer of blubber attached, a special delicacy. It is called *maktak,* or *muktuk,* and it is eaten raw. In the areas of Point Hope, Wainwright, and Point Barrow, the Eskimo umiaks are brought out in the early spring each year for repairs, and a period of great excitement and entertainment for the villagers is begun. Boats are fitted, gear is readied, and the umiaks take to the open waters. Luck and the weather will decide whether many or no whales will be taken, and the outcome is of course of vital concern to the villagers. But just as important is the appeal of whaling itself as the hunters confront its dangers, accept its challenges, and display, both individually and in groups, their remarkable seamanship and skill.

Chapter Three

Capitals Old and New

Who was responsible for our purchase of Alaska? Most historians give credit to William Henry Seward, our Secretary of State under Lincoln. Seward, whose far-sightedness is just beginning to be appreciated, reasoned that in order to properly defend the United States we needed Alaska to dominate the North Pacific, and Greenland and Iceland to dominate the North Atlantic. He advocated that we buy Greenland and Iceland from Denmark and Alaska from Russia; but he succeeded only with the Russian part of his plan. Negotiations were opened with Russia for the purchase of Alaska, a price of $7,200,000 agreed upon, and at 4:00 A.M., March 30, 1867, the Treaty of Purchase was signed by Secretary Seward, acting for us, and by Baron de Stoeckl, acting for Russia.

At the time of the purchase the capital of Russian America, as it was called then, was Sitka. To this day it remains the most Russian city in the state. Everywhere in Sitka are reminders that it was once a thriving Imperial metropolis, with a gay social life, indeed, it was a cultural center for the entire

Sitka, the former capital of Alaska.

northwest coast. This city, which all Sitkans, and many non-Sitkans, consider the most picturesque in Alaska, was founded in 1799 when a Siberian trader, Alexander Baranof, moved there from Kodiak Island. He arrived with thirty Russians, several hundred Aleuts, and a charter from the Russian America Company, which had exclusive rights to all profits that might be derived from any resource whatsoever in the Russian colony. Baranof was under orders to stop the trade in furs and ivory being carried on by other nations. He was also to protect the Indians' lives and property, to feed them in time of disaster, to educate their children, and if possible, save their souls.

The Indians, unaware of this intended kindness, resisted the newcomers vigorously. Ten of the thirty Russians had constantly to stand on guard. The local people would capture and kill any single man or small group of Russians. In 1802 when Baranof was away visiting Kodiak Island, the Indians captured the post, killing all the men and taking the women and children prisoners. Baranof returned in 1804 and rebuilt the village, naming it New Archangel. The Tlingit Indian word, Sitka, which means the "best place," had long been in use, however, and the new name did not stick. The hostility between the Indians and the whites continued until as late as 1855 when a battle showed a score in dead and wounded of 21 Russians and 60 Indians.

At the end of the eighteenth century, while San Francisco was still a mission, Sitka became the largest settlement on the entire Pacific Coast, a center of trade and civilization. Into the exquisite Bay of Sitka, peppered with tiny spruce-covered islets and dominated by towering Mt. Edgecumbe, came clipper ships from New England stopping off on their way to China, English trading ships, ships from Kronstadt on the Baltic, Spanish ships, French ships. Here Yankee traders matched wits with Tlingit Indians, the Yankees frequently getting the worst of the bargain. It was the gayest, most brilliant city of a huge wilderness empire.

On October 18, 1867, Sitka witnessed the dramatic formal ceremonies which transferred possession of Alaska from Russia to the United States. Russian soldiers in dark red-trimmed uniforms and United States troops in full dress stood at attention in front of the governor's castle, making a brave show despite the rain. The Commissioner of the Imperial Ruler of all the Russias said the necessary words and the U.S. Commissioner received the land for its new owners. The Russian flag was lowered and the American flag raised in its place, to the accompaniment of tears from the Russian ladies and salutes from the batteries and ships' guns in the harbor. Later most of the Russian families returned to Russia; only a few remained, and their descendents still live in Sitka.

St. Michael's Cathedral, Russian Orthodox church. Its bells, and many of those for California missions, were cast in Sitka.

Reminders of Sitka's Russian past turn up at Easter time, when decorated eggs are traded, and *kulich*, a sweet holiday bread, is eaten. Two Christmases are celebrated, one at the usual time, the other according to the Russian calendar. Another reason for the continuation of some old Russian customs is that Sitka remains the spiritual center of the Russian Orthodox Church in Alaska. At St. Michael's Cathedral, where services are still held in Russian, beautiful old icons and other religious treasures are housed.

Today Sitka is a modern town of more than two thousand, famous for the beauty of its natural setting and its pleasantly mild climate. Except for the airways, you approach Sitka only from the sea, through a beautiful narrow channel that runs between it and Japonski Island, location of the Alaska Native Service Mount Edgecumbe Boarding School. Here you see for the first time the peak of Mount Edgecumbe, an extinct volcano often compared to Fujiyama. The innumerable little green islands that surround the old capital offer calm lagoons for sailing, or sheltered landing places for pontoon planes. The famous Sheldon Jackson School and Junior College, named for the Presbyterian missionary and educator, is at Sitka. Its museum contains interesting Indian and Eskimo exhibits.

Sitka has hotels, a radio station, a fine government hospital, a library, cold storage plant, and the famous Pioneers Home for aged sourdoughs, built on the old Russian parade ground. A new pulp mill, which will employ seven hundred people, was nearing completion in 1958. Older residents hope it will not change Sitka's personality; it is sure to add to its prosperity.

Sitka National Monument Park has a splendid collection of totem poles. Eighteen in number, they were gathered from many parts of Alaska for an exhibit in the 1904 St. Louis Exposition. When the fair was over, Alaska's Governor John

Visitors to Alaska may see totem poles at Ketchikan, Sitka and other places.

Brady succeeded in having them returned to Alaska and placed in Indian River Park, which later became a national park.

After the purchase, Sitka remained the capital of Alaska until 1900, when the rapidly growing city of Juneau was named as the new seat of government. Governor Brady and the executive offices remained in Sitka until 1906, thereafter the new governor took up his duties in Juneau.

Juneau, still the capital, stands on Gastineau Channel at the water's edge, framed by the steep, timbered slopes of Mount Juneau and Mount Roberts, which tower above the

Juneau, with her twin city, Douglas, across the Channel.

city. There is so little space between the mountains' edge and the water that one wonders how a town came to be built on this particular spot. The answer is easily found—gold. Juneau's history, like that of other places in the state, begins with the discovery of the yellow metal. Two prospectors, Harris and Juneau, found gold at Silver Bow Basin in 1880, and before the next spring arrived, more than a hundred men were camped at the site. This was the first gold rush on Alaskan soil. Harris and Juneau disagreed for two years about naming their camp and finally a town meeting of miners was held so that a decision might be reached. A compromise was effected by calling the town Juneau and the district Harrisburg.

From the time of the United States purchase until 1897 there was a black period of lawlessness in Alaska's history. With no civil law or administration for maintaining order, murder, burglary, and drunkenness were the order of the day. The gold stampeders in the late 1890's and 1900's, although without civil authority, created their own form of local self-government, on the order of New England town meetings. Together with such sporadic administration as was possible through the Army, Navy and Custom Service, this served until 1912, when the Alaskan Legislature was created.

Gold mining continued to be the chief industry in Juneau for more than half a century, until, when the price of gold was fixed by the Federal Government and mining costs rose steadily, it no longer paid. The huge Alaska Juneau Mine, once the largest gold mining operation in the world, reckoning by tonnage, stands silent and empty today. It once employed almost a thousand men and had an annual payroll of more than a million dollars. The only gold mining in the Juneau area today is the reworking of old slag heaps, to gather up the tiny bits of valuable ore that escaped the original operations.

Juneau's connections with other cities in Alaska are by water and air, except for Douglas. Douglas is her twin city; it stands on a wooded island across a narrow channel spanned by a bridge.

Juneau,
a modern city,
has a dramatic setting,
perched on a narrow
ledge between Mount
Juneau and the deep
waters of Gastineau
Channel.

There is a splendid harbor at Juneau, crowded in season by salmon and halibut fishing vessels, with excellent docking facilities. This is a modern town with tall buildings set on steep hills, reminding one of San Francisco. Administrative offices of

the Federal Government are housed in a many-storied build-ing, in which there is a fascinating Alaskan museum. The fa-vorite gathering place for legislators, visitors, and townfolk is the coffee shop of the Baranof Hotel, where issues are hotly debated and many social and business matters settled.

Juneau has a modern airport, with a connecting automobile road running through another of Alaska's startling landscapes. Here are spectacular mountains, brilliant glaciers glistening in the sun, set against dark green, tree-covered slopes, all contributing to a colorful scene of splendor. Nearby Menden-hall Glacier, one of the few in the world accessible by auto-mobile road, is a seventeen-mile-long ice stream that provides an important tourist attraction, but is also enjoyed and thor-oughly explored by native Juneauites. On a sunny day its crevasses reflect the strong blues of sky and surrounding water. In Auk Lake outside Juneau you may swim comfortably with-in sight of a white glacier!

Auk Lake with Mendenhall Glacier in the background.

Chief Shake was a famous leader of the Tlingit Indians.

Chapter Four

The First Families

All the "first families" of Alaska were originally Eskimos or other Indians. In the southeastern part of the country lived the Tlingit Indians with a considerable unwritten literature and a wealthy, aristocratic society that included slavery and the potlatch.

The potlatch was a public celebration, where, to the accompaniment of singing, dancing, dramatic recitations, and feasting, a man would give away rich gifts to all. Here a new totem pole would be dedicated, marriages celebrated, claims and proclamations announced, and fine clothes displayed. At first glance, it would seem to be a scheme for pauperization, for a chief might give away most of his possessions, including huge dug-out canoes and valuable Chilkat blankets. But a careful tally was kept of all presents and rigid etiquette demanded that all gifts be returned with interest, which might run as high as 100 per cent. In effect, the potlatch was a banking system, and a form of insurance, investment, social security, and credit circulation. If a man died, the gift was owed to

47

his heirs. To avoid payment was unthinkable. Traditionally, all gifts were supposed to be of the finest workmanship, made from the best materials. So the potlatch stimulated every form of art to its highest pitch, whether in weaving of mats, baskets, and blankets, or the carving of jewelry, gift boxes, canoes, or totem poles.

Totem poles, usually placed at the entrance to a man's home, commemorated a special event; or, through animal symbols, the family totem, or family tree. Most of the surviving poles in Alaska have been preserved and carefully restored. Fine examples may be seen at Sitka National Monument Park, at Saxman Park outside Ketchikan, and elsewhere. These great works of native art, once ignored and permitted to decay, are now widely appreciated, especially by Alaskans and by visiting art experts. During the tourist season, they are among the most photographed items in the land.

The Tlingits, who once numbered between seven and eight thousand, are about half that number now. The decrease of this formerly warlike nation has been due, in recent years, more to absorption by other groups than to disease.

In addition to the Tlingits, Alaska's Panhandle has two other important Indian groups: about seven or eight hundred Tsimshians and a thousand Haidas. The prosperous Tsimshians, who live mostly at Metlakatla, and the Haidas, whose fathers migrated from British Columbia about four or five hundred years ago, are small segments of large tribes still living in Canada. These, as well as the Tlingits, had a high culture, fine houses, and a stratified society in the days of their former glory. The Eyak Indians, who controlled the copper trade, and whose central point was at Cordova, have now disappeared, through absorption by other groups.

Little remains of the old Indian cultures. The sons of great warriors now work in modern canneries and pulp mills, or for shipping and airline companies. Most of their ancient, highly developed craft skills have been forgotten, but a few have been revived for souvenir-hungry visitors to Alaska. Totem poles are being carved again, but in miniature form, for sale, and without the semi-religious feeling that used to accompany their carving, presentation, and possession.

The universally popular Eskimos are the largest group of native people in Alaska. After a long and almost disastrous population decline, they are beginning to increase, and in 1958 numbered about 18,000. They are an able-bodied, good-humored, self-reliant, clever people who have dwelt, for the last four or five thousand years, along the shores of the Arctic and Bering Seas, as well as in the river deltas and in some cases up the river valleys, especially along the Colville, Noatak, Kobuk, and Kuskokwim. They have always been a hunting people, following the fish and game animals with the seasons, but usually remaining in one general area. They hunted caribou, mountain sheep and moose on the land; polar bear, seal, walrus, and whale at sea. Except for city dwellers, like the five hundred who live in Fairbanks, most Eskimos still derive at least part of their living from the same animals hunted by their ancestors.

To some extent the Eskimos have always been fishermen, particularly on the Bering coast. Through the influence of the Russian American Company, of the Hudson's Bay Company, and of the Free Traders (as the independent competitors of the great fur trading companies were called), they became fur trappers as well.

North of the Arctic Circle the majority of the Eskimos lived, for at least part of the year, on or near the coast. On the great inland prairie the population is now sparse; only fifty years ago it was inhabited by ten or perhaps twenty times as many Eskimos as now. Then and earlier, coastal folk depended

Eskimos on back of a small white whale, or beluga.

Eskimo boy with fish drying racks.

chiefly on seal and whale for food, those of the interior on caribou, supplemented by birds, and fish from the inland lakes and rivers. In the mountains a comparatively few lived mainly on sheep.

Seal, walrus, and whale oil provided coastal Eskimos with fuel and light. The inlanders used spruce, alder, and willow for fuel, and in their camps burned caribou tallow for light, or oil purchased from the coastal people in exchange for caribou hides and sheepskins. Once a year, oftenest in late winter, they would come down to the sea to hunt seals, to visit, and to trade.

Since their culture was so perfectly adapted to the climate of the Arctic, we tend to think of Eskimos as primarily an arctic people. But according to Ivar Skarland, Professor of Anthropology at the University of Alaska, more Eskimos now live south of the latitude of Fairbanks, than north of it. With the population center actually south of the Yukon River, Alaska's Eskimos may be correctly described today as a *generally* subarctic people.

The western and southern coasts of Alaska were in fairly close touch with the Russians, and with other white men, in the eighteenth century, and the interior similarly in the nineteenth. The north coast had sporadic whalers a hundred years ago but no resident trader until Charles D. Brower settled at Barrow in 1885, where his son still runs his famous trading post. Generally throughout Alaska, missionaries followed close on the heels of the traders.

The whalers and traders needed fresh meat for food and to ward off the dreaded scurvy. They had never heard of vitamins, but sea captains knew if they had fresh meat they and their crews would remain in good health. So they offered lures of every sort to get the Eskimos to hunt for them.

Soon after the first contact between the two peoples, Alaskan natives began to die in great numbers from diseases brought in by the whites. This was no doubt so throughout Alaska, but we know the story best from the Eskimos. The deadliness of the illnesses was due to their newness. No ancestor of an Eskimo had ever been exposed to any of them; therefore none had a natural immunity.

It is commonly believed that the worst killer that ever swept the natives of the New World was smallpox. But insofar as we know the history of Alaska, the deadliest scourge was measles. There was an epidemic around the turn of the century which killed not less than one quarter of the people in any village we know about. This epidemic, according to a report we believe authentic, killed nearly 99 per cent in one village, the only survivor being a girl of about six.

The second epidemic, a few years later, may have killed from 10 to 20 per cent, the third killed only a few, and now the danger of measles to the Eskimos is not much greater than to us. Those who survived the first and second epidemics had an immunity against measles. Similar death rates from measles have been reported from tropical islands of the Pacific. Indeed a high mortality rate has been reported wherever measles had been previously unknown.

After measles, tuberculosis became the deadliest Eskimo disease, and held the lead for decades. The death rate rose to fourteen times that in the rest of the United States. Recently this appalling ratio was reduced through Public Health Service measures, new drugs, and additional hospitals. Some think Eskimos always had tuberculosis but that it was kept in check by their wholesome food and way of life. Others think, and this is now becoming the majority view, that Eskimos never had tuberculosis until it was introduced in historic times. Only very recently, middle-ear infections and mastoiditis have surpassed tuberculosis as the major health problem among Alaska natives.

Under their "primitive" way of life Eskimos were free of many diseases which plague the white man. Apparently they formerly never had tooth decay, cancer, scurvy, or beri-beri. As they shifted to the white man's way of life they acquired his diseases too, and now Eskimo teeth are as badly decayed as ours, and cancer is reported to be increasing.

One great benefit the whites brought to the Eskimos was the reduction of the death rate at childbirth for both mothers and children. Among primitive Eskimos it was not permissible for anyone to be present when a child was being born. The most custom permitted was that a woman's mother might be outside the house, shouting advice in to her daughter. In other areas, even this was taboo. But the Eskimos had one advantage, even in childbirth cases; the bacteria which cause infections, including "blood poisoning," were rare or absent. In the Arctic and sub-Arctic, almost every wound was formerly a clean wound. There was less need for iodine in the medicine kit.

The Eskimos and Indians of Alaska used to be wards of the Government. They had no rights of citizenship, but the Government was pledged to look after their welfare. In 1924 an Act of Congress provided that "all non-citizen Indians, born within the territorial limits of the United States, shall be citizens," and that the granting of citizenship shall not in any way affect the right of an Indian to tribal or other property. Some have contended that the Eskimos are not Indians, and would not come under this law, but it has been ruled that the law does apply to them. It would be strange if the law did not, for biologically and anthropologically they are of the same race.

Until their contact with Europeans, when births began to be recorded by missionaries and school teachers, the Eskimos did not know how old they were, except in a vague way, and considered it unimportant. They did not reckon age by years but by terms like our "infant," "child," "youth," "adult." This was a matter of social outlook, though it has been said by whites that the Eskimos had trouble with counting. That idea cannot have come from any close knowledge of the Alaska Eskimos. Except for imbeciles, of whom they have some just as we do, you would never have met anyone who couldn't count to four hundred. Primitive Eskimos counted by twenties, using both fingers and toes, where we use only the fingers; so that what corresponds to our hundred, ten times ten, is for them four hundred, twenty times twenty. Occasionally some Eskimo might tell you that it was not possible to count higher than four hundred, but if you pressed him he could usually devise an extension. It was no more logically necessary for them to stop at four hundred than it is for us to stop at one hundred.

To measure distance the Eskimos had nothing like our miles, but reckoned a journey in fractions of a day. If it was more than two days, they usually spoke in number of days. True, many whites in Alaska have had the impression that Eskimos reckoned journeys by sleeps, one sleep being two days, two sleeps three days, and so on. But this appears to be an idea which the whites brought with them, perhaps having derived it from youthful enjoyment of stories by James Fenimore Cooper. The Eskimos had no trouble in getting the Fenimore Cooper idea, and now there are many of them who, even among themselves, will reckon a journey in sleeps.

An idea, or at least a word, which they did not have was "year." They spoke of spring, summer, autumn, and winter, and they reckoned years either in winters or in summers.

They had months in the sense of moons, and usually knew

that there were thirteen in the complete cycle. But some of them would tell you that there were eight moons, nine moons, ten moons, according to what part of Alaska you were in, and then they would give the moonless period, which would be the summer, when the night was so bright that the moon could not be seen.

One of the strangest ideas to an Eskimo is that of our cardinal or compass points. Their directional thinking is not governed by the sun, but rather by the shoreline, for most of them were coastal people. So their directional phrases are "up the coast," "down the coast," "inland," and "out to sea." This has been confusing to those whites who did not know the language

An Eskimo family.

thoroughly, and you find in the vocabularies of Eskimo words copied down by the average traveler an entry stating *nigerk* is a west wind, a south wind, and a north wind. *Nigerk* actually means a wind that blows up the coast. Similarly *kanangnak* which has many meanings in published vocabularies, has only one meaning to the Eskimos. It is a wind from the sea which may be north, south, east, or west, according to where you are. *Pingangnak* is a wind from the land, from "up there."

The Eskimo language is perhaps the hardest of all languages in the world to acquire. The only whites who really learn it are a few missionaries who have been studious and who have lived long in the country, a half-dozen scientists, and a few who have married Eskimo women. Only from them can you get a discriminating understanding of how the Eskimos think and of what ideas are and are not within their scheme.

Eskimos are quick-witted and intelligent, to an extent well above the average, showing a remarkable capacity for appreciating and learning useful things, especially the mechanical arts.

One explorer tells of an Eskimo who possessed a dollar watch, which stopped after two years of use. Its owner proceeded to open the back of it and take it apart, piece by piece. After carefully cleaning each part he put it back together again so that it worked, although he had never in his life taken a watch apart. Equally remarkable tales are told of their ingenuity in repairing outboard motor engines they have never seen before, to the astonishment of people who have thought of them vaguely as a "primitive" people.

Eskimos in Alaska never used the snow house, (see p. 98), but formerly built their houses of earth. North of the tree line, driftwood was substituted for local spruce to make the frames; and in some places the large bones of whales were used. In spring the Eskimo traditionally left his house to spend the summer in a tent. In the old days the tent was of skins; now it is apt to be of canvas.

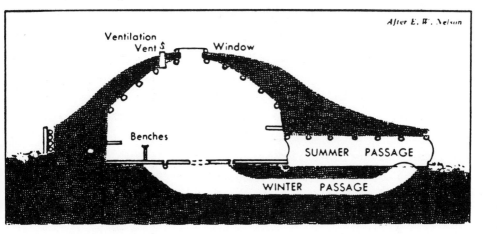

After E. W. Nelson

Ventilation
Vent

Window

Benches

SUMMER PASSAGE

WINTER PASSAGE

This schematic drawing shows how the air-capture principle is used in an Alaskan earth-and-wood house. In summer, the gut window is removed and a ground-level entrance is used. In winter, these are both closed and the house is entered through a passage by which bouyant warm air cannot escape. This passage is never closed all winter, unless by just a grid to keep out dogs.

One of the Eskimo's remarkable inventions was the way he used gravity in his house to keep the cold out and the warmth in. Winter houses, as made on the north coast of Alaska, had thick earth walls and were always entered from below. The top of the door was always lower than the floor, and usually at the end of an alleyway. You entered the house by going down into a passage and up into the house at the other end. So long as the door was lower than the floor, it never needed to be shut, even at 50° below zero. For cold air is heavier than warm air, and cannot rise *upwards* into a house already filled with warm air. Fresh air was provided by a small ventilator about four inches in diameter in the roof of the house. Cold air could enter from the door below only as warm air was permitted to escape through the ceiling vent. By widening or narrowing this vent, the Eskimo regulated the amount of heated air permitted to escape and cold air permitted to enter, thus controlling both the temperature and the ventilation of his house. If the house were too warm—and a normal temperature for an Eskimo house might be 80° or 90°—the ventilator was opened wide; if too cool, it would be partially closed. A house with one room, big enough for two average families, needed only three seal oil lamps to keep the temperature at what we would consider more like a Turkish bath than a comfortable room temperature. (See drawing on p. 57.)

The First Families

The beach of an old Eskimo village was always its main plaza, the equivalent of our small village green, or common. It was the center of traffic and activity both in summer and winter. From the beach the hunter went sealing in his graceful kayak, and it was to the beach he returned. If successful, he was surrounded by interested and helpful neighbors. The animal would often be skinned and, if large, divided on the beach. Here, too, families starting off on a journey would pile

The beach of an old Eskimo village was its main thoroughfare both in summer and in winter.

their children, dogs, and household gear in the family umiak and wave a cheerful farewell as they paddled off. In winter, dog teams and sledges would depart and return via the beach.

Eskimos held views almost the opposite of ours about water and ice. To them ice was something friendly on which they could walk and hunt, which protected them from the treacherous waters below. We usually think of the water as being safe, the ice as treacherous. Eskimos seldom learned to swim. The waters of the Arctic Sea and Bering Sea are too cold, the mosquitoes too many and too hungry. Only children take off their boots and socks and go wading in the shallow water off the beach, and that only in the hottest weather.

The Eskimo hunting canoe, the kayak, is no doubt the most seaworthy craft of its size. The spruce driftwood frames are shaped by hand. The pieces, instead of being nailed together, are lashed with wet rawhide, which draws tight as it dries. The sealskin covering fully envelops the boat except for a round deck opening just large enough to receive a man.

In some districts the boat's "manhole" merely fits the hunter's body rather snugly so as to give water little chance to enter; properly, the opening has a raised edge to which the Eskimo lashes the hem of his waterproof coat so that paddler and canoe become one. Water is prevented from entering not merely through the manhole but also through the sleeves and neck of the coat, which are tightly lashed. This hooded raincoat is made from animal intestines, which are dried and sewn together to make a translucent, waterproof slicker.

The kayak is about as steady on rough water as a man on a swaying tightrope. Its seaworthiness lies in the skill of the kayaker with his long double paddle, and in the boat and boatman being a single unit.

Getting in and out of a kayak is a tricky art, and few white men can manage it without a ducking. It is accomplished by

Eskimo boat frames were formerly shaped from driftwood, now imported lumber is often used.

A kayak overturns easily but a good kayaker can right it with equal ease.

An expert kayaker must start his training early. Father is usually teacher—here he demonstrates first lessons in paddling.

placing a pike pole or paddle across the boat, with the other end resting on ice or on the beach. When a steady balance has been achieved, the kayaker ventures in or out. But don't try it on the basis of these instructions!

The pike pole is a very useful implement. It is used for cutting ice, for pulling wounded game within reach, and for propelling the kayak in shallow water.

When an Eskimo boy is about twelve years old, his father will begin to teach him the difficult technique of handling a kayak, in those areas where they are still used. Long before this time, probably when he was six or seven, he learned to use a gun. He has killed small game and, if lucky, a seal. With his father he has gone on trips by dog team and perhaps made a short sledge journey or two by himself. But a kayak, unless expertly handled, is extremely dangerous. A boy must be serious-minded and industrious to master the art of handling this marvelous little craft, for a mishap may end in drowning.

Instructions usually begin in a quiet lagoon sheltered from the rough surf. The kayak is so placed on the beach that while afloat on a few inches of water it can still be reached from dry land. The father then gets into the kayak and explains how to hold and manipulate the paddle, demonstrating each step as he tells of it. When this is thoroughly understood, father and son change places and while the father holds on to the kayak, the boy imitates the motions of paddling. Step by step each maneuver is rehearsed and memorized before the boy takes to the water alone. Even then he is carefully watched and never goes far from shore at first. It takes years of practice to become an expert kayaker but once the skill is acquired, kayak and paddler become practically unsinkable.

Accidents do occur in kayaks, but death usually results not from the kayak overturning once, because a good kayaker can right himself half a dozen times easily, but from the paddler being so fatigued from repeated capsizing that he is unable to right his boat.

While the kayak is a greater marvel of design, nearly the same admiration is due the larger umiak. This Eskimo boat, also skin-covered, is a dory type of craft, and like a dory, extremely seaworthy and capable of long voyages in rough weather. The average umiak is thirty-five or forty feet long, can transport a two-ton load, yet is light enough for a man and his partner to carry. It is so strong and well fitted for rough handling that the Yankee shore whalers of northwestern Alaska, toward the end of the nineteenth century, exchanged their New Bedford whaleboats for umiaks in pursuing the bowhead whale. An ordinary wooden whaleboat is easily damaged even by small fragments of floating ice, while an umiak going at the same speed will not be harmed at all. A skin boat behaves somewhat like a football when it is struck. A thump is followed by a bouncy rebound. Should a blow be severe, the result might be a cracked rib that can be replaced at leisure, while a hole in the skin is easily patched with needle and thread.

Because it is light, has a flat bottom, and draws only a few inches of water, an umiak can venture safely into shallow places where ordinary boats are unable to navigate.

In summer, to prevent the skin covering of an umiak from decaying, it must be taken out of the water and dried at least every four days—preferably every three. This is easily accomplished. When a party camps for the night, the boat is taken out of the water and tilted on edge. If the weather is fair, the skins will be dry in the morning.

Before the era of the airplane and tractor-pulled sledge trains, a dog sled was the only winter means of overland transportation in many parts of Alaska. As long as the ground was snow-covered, which might be for seven months of the year, dog teams were used by trappers, hunters and mail car-

A skin covered umiak is light for its size and easily carried. Here Eskimo whalers are carrying theirs to an open lead. All wear goggles to prevent snowblindness.

riers. Although still used, for sport racing now as well as utility, their numbers decrease each year.

The so-called pure bred Husky dog is a recent development by white men who carefully breed only dogs of a certain height, color, and fur, deciding beforehand the characteristics desired. These dogs, usually white and large, are commonly bred and trained in Maine and New Hampshire, and are shipped to the Arctic. They are also used extensively by explorers both in the Arctic and Antarctic.

Some early fur traders sent out by the Hudson's Bay Company to northern Canada were cockney Englishmen who dropped their *h's* and inserted others where they didn't belong. They called Eskimos "Heskimos." An Eskimo dog was a "Heskimo" dog. "Heskimo" was soon shortened to "Hesky," which eventually became "Husky."

The sled dog is hero of many a dangerous journey. The close, tender companionship and near-human understanding that a well-treated team of dogs offers its master is beyond the talents of most authors to describe. Hard-working, willing and loyal, whether well-fed or half-starved, they work in winter pulling, and in summer as pack animals. If food is short, these dogs are first to have their rations cut. Yet history tells us that many a starving dog has died in its traces, pulling with its last breath.

Once upon a time there probably *was* such a thing as a pure bred Eskimo dog, but almost the first Europeans who reached the North brought with them dogs which were bred with Eskimo dogs. Today only two distinctions can be made. There are the small Siberian sled dogs, often pure white or black and white, sometimes with milky blue eyes, and the ordinary Eskimo dogs which are really mongrels and may be of almost any size or color. During the Gold Rush, hundreds of dogs of various breeds were brought into the country, ranging down from St. Bernards and Newfoundlands. Many Alaska Eskimo dogs still show traces of those breeds.

Wintertime, when it is a little too dark to do any real hunting, becomes holiday time for those Eskimos who still live as they did in earlier days. Much of the dark season is spent making sledge journeys to visit back and forth with friends. Eskimo dog teams, once small, may now number thirteen or even more, varying with the wealth of the owner and the fashion in a given area. A lead dog is not necessarily the strongest member of a team, but he is usually the most intelligent, for he must interpret the driver's commands. Spirit is the mark of the

Sled dogs curl up to sleep in the snow.

leader, who may be of either sex and any size. When a litter of pups is large enough, the fuzzy little balls of fur are allowed to romp and run alongside a trained team. The puppy that runs ahead and tries to stay in front is marked as a future lead dog. At least, many Alaskans say it is as simple as that.

Thanks to his superior nose, a good leader can often find a trail, made invisible by drifting snow, and guide a lost driver safely home. Lazy dogs are rare, but not unknown. Most sled dogs love to pull, and yelp excitedly as they are harnessed for a trip much as a city dog dances with anticipation when his master appears with a leash that promises an outing.

Helping the dogs cross a difficult place.

Sled dogs are fed once a day and their ration usually is a dried salmon, but they will eat almost anything if they are used to it, seal, caribou or goose. Dog fights which break out must be stopped immediately, for they may result in the death or maiming of a valuable dog. For this reason dogs are seldom allowed to run loose. After a day's work, they are tethered to stakes, out of reach of each other. Good sled dogs are workers rather than pets; for doing their particular job these tough. handsome beasts are unsurpassed.

Eskimo sleds can carry from five hundred to a thousand pounds of load. But an Eskimo, unless ill, will never ride on the sled. He is much more likely to be up front giving the dogs a hand over a rough spot where the pulling is hard. In extremely cold weather, if the sled is allowed to stop, the runners will freeze fast in the snow. Then the sled must be rocked loose with a gee pole. Among the innovations introduced by white men is a kind of rude brake on the back of the sled. It will not stop a runaway team, but is useful for slowing the sled when going downhill.

Some think Eskimos were able to survive in the Arctic and "endure the terrific cold" because they hardened themselves to it, and so could stand it better than white men. But formerly Eskimos never endured or suffered cold; they protected themselves from it in many ingenious ways. They wore truly marvelous, cold-proof clothing which kept them warm however extreme the cold. An Eskimo in his old-style clothing could don a ten-pound caribou skin outfit in January and sit still comfortably outdoors all afternoon while fishing through the ice at 50° below zero. Compare this with our average city dweller's midwinter costume in which he would soon freeze to death if he didn't keep moving, at temperatures a good deal higher than 50° below.

A Point Hope Eskimo youth in his coat which has the skin side outside and the fur side inside.

Before the white man's influence became strong, Eskimo cold-weather dress consisted of two suits of caribou skin; the inner one was worn with the fur side in, and the outer with the fur side out. Each suit was made up of coat, or *attigi*, and breeches which tied about the waist with a drawstring, for there are no buttons or buttonholes on truly Eskimo clothing. Both undershirt and outer coat had hoods exposing the cheeks and forehead but protecting the ears. Boots and mittens completed the costume. Both inner and outer coats were worn loose, outside the trousers. If the weather became so windy that the garment flapped, a belt was passed around the under-coat, preventing the cool air from coming up inside.

It is not enough to own a suit of Eskimo clothing to insure comfortable protection from the cold. It is also necessary to know how to wear it and take care of it. Dry snow and hoar-frost must always be carefully removed before entering a warm house.

When caribou skins have been dried and scraped they are soft and free from odors. Then the highly skilled Eskimo women fashion them into garments, each of which is a tailor-made work of art. Eskimo seamstresses make what is probably the only truly waterproof seam in the world. Our bootmakers think a seam cannot be waterproof and usually rub oil or wax into their needle holes. But if an Eskimo sewer sees you rubbing oil on her boot seam she will feel insulted. When a waterboot is finished she inflates it like a balloon, twists the mouth, and waits for a few minutes to see if any air is escaping. She holds the seam to her cheek to detect the slightest leak of air, or near a lamp or candle flame to notice the slightest flicker. Caribou sinew was originally used for thread. When a new pair of boots was about to be worn they would be dampened and the sinew would swell, making the seam tighter than ever.

Observing the white people's fashions, Eskimos were quick to adopt first one, then another item of their clothes. Eventually the miracle of the mail-order catalogue reached every Eskimo, however remote. Summer dress throughout the Eskimo world then underwent a change. Formerly skin clothing was worn the year round—it was all they had. Now cotton dresses and shirts, rubber boots, blue jeans, and plaid lumber jackets are as popular with them as with us. For summer wear our clothing is more comfortable than theirs; but in winter theirs is far better than ours. Nothing we can offer is nearly as good in extreme cold as an Eskimo caribou skin coat, or an Eskimo-style sealskin waterboot. These two items at least seem destined to survive every onslaught of fashion. An important reason for Eskimos to adopt our clothing is that many now work for wages and have no time to hunt caribou and seals: so there are no skins for making clothing.

Eskimo mothers used to, and many still do, carry their babies on their backs inside their coats, the child sitting pick-a-back fashion with its little legs around the mother's waist. A belt to prevent it from slipping down was passed under the child in back, brought forward and fastened in front over the mother's breast (see page 73). If the child was young, it was naked and completely hidden from view inside the coat. If older, and the weather mild, it might be lightly clad and its head might protrude from the top of the coat.

Unless his parents are getting all too disagreeably "civilized," an Eskimo child is never punished. The reason is not that Eskimos love their children more than other parents, but rather what they used to believe about the soul.

According to their ancient theory, a child is born with a soul and a body that are equally small and weak. It seemed obvious to an Eskimo that the child would never get along if it did not have a more experienced and wiser soul to look after it.

Eskimo mother and child.

So the first thing a mother did after her child was born was to pronounce a spell and summon the spirit of some person who had recently died.

The Eskimos have no sex indication in their language. They have no pronouns like "he" or "she" in English; they have no sex inflexion for adjectives and nouns such as you find in Latin or German. This may be why it made no difference in their thinking whether the spirit summoned was that of a man or woman. In some districts it had to be the spirit of a near relative who had recently died. In another area it might be the spirit of the last person who had died, irrespective of relationship.

It was the Eskimo view of the spirits of the dead that they are strongest just after they first enter the newborn child, and gradually become weaker as the child grows up. Correspondingly, the inborn soul of the child is thought to be weakest at birth and gradually becomes stronger. So Eskimos believed that when a child is very young its thinking is done for it exclusively by the soul of the dead person, the child's inborn soul having little or no control. If, for instance, a child cried for the scissors it was, in Eskimo opinion, the judgment of the guardian soul that the child ought to have the scissors.

This gave the parents two reasons for yielding. In the first place, who are they to think that they are wiser than the guardian spirit? And, anyhow, if they refused they would offend the guardian, which would thereupon leave the child. With nothing but its own incompetent soul to take care of it, the baby would suffer one misfortune after another. If a man's ears stuck out at the wrong angle or if his nose had a strange shape it was usual to hear people remark that his parents must have punished him when he was young.

According to the old Eskimo way of thinking, during the first few years of a child's life, you were distinctly speaking to the soul of the dead when you addressed the child. Therefore it was customary for those related to the dead to address a baby in terms of that relationship. For instance, if my grandmother's soul had been given to a small boy, I would call him "grandmother" whenever I spoke to him, or about him. A mother talking to her baby girl might call her "father," if it was her father's soul which had been given to her daughter.

While Eskimos in general are now Christian and not supposed to believe in guardian spirits, it remains true to this day that Eskimo children are practically never punished physically or forbidden anything.

It is commonly believed that primitive people have simple languages, but the linguists who spend their lives studying speech tell us the opposite is often true. This is confirmed by the Eskimo language, which (as we said earlier) some believe to be the hardest language in the world to learn. The active daily vocabulary has more than ten thousand words, most of which are nouns and verbs. Adjective and adverb meanings are supplied by inflexion. The inflexions are so numerous and complicated that one noun can be written in more than a thousand forms, each with a separate, precise meaning of its own. A verb can have even more forms than a noun!

The structure of Eskimo is so different from English that you must learn a new way of thinking as well as a new vocabulary if you want to speak the language. This will not be true if you are a Finn, a Lapp, or a Hungarian; for structurally your language would be related to Eskimo.

For instance, the average American, who wants to learn the language, seeks out an Eskimo who speaks English and, taking care not to be misunderstood, he will hold a knife in his hand and ask, "What is your word for 'knife'?" The Eskimo will answer *"savik"*; "And what is your word for 'big'?" is the next question, whereupon the answer, in Colville River dialect, will

be *"angirok."* "Now," thinks the white man, "I know how to
say 'big knife,' " but as a matter of fact he doesn't know at all,
for the Eskimo does not say "big knife" by attaching the adjective for "big" to the word for "knife." Instead he inflects the
word for knife by adding a syllable, in this case *pa* which
means big. A big knife is not as we might think *"savik angirok"*
or *"angirok savik"*; it is *"savipak."* We are accustomed to
prefixes and suffixes; the Eskimos also use *in*fixes. That is, they
take a word apart and insert a syllable in the middle (rather
than at the beginning or end), to alter the meaning.

There are nine cases in Eskimo and they, as in Greek, have
singular, dual, and plural forms, giving you theoretically
twenty-seven variants of a word, before you add any infixes.
(However it is difficult to make out nine forms in the dual.)

To get an idea of how the inflexions work, take the word
iglu which means a temporary or permanent shelter of any
sort. *Iglupak*, means a large house; *iglunguak*, a make-believe
or playhouse; *iglorak*, a wooden house; *iglukuk*, a ruined
house; *igluliak*, a house that someone built; *iglulik*, that which
contains houses, as an island which is inhabited; *iglutun*, like
a house, and so on for several hundred variants of the one
word *iglu*.

The noun is simple compared with the verb. It is probable
that no man has ever worked out the number of possible different ways in which a single Eskimo verb may be used, but an
experienced Eskimo linguist has estimated it at a minimum of
three thousand.

With only this hint of an explanation, it may no longer appear strange that some white men who have lived in the area
twenty or thirty years, and are married to Eskimo women, cannot understand what their wives are saying when they talk to
the children.

Because Eskimo has proved too difficult for all the neighbor

Eskimos do rub noses! But it is an affectionate gesture generally used between young children and older women.

peoples, whether forest Indians or whites, there has grown up a trade language, a jargon or pidgin, wherever an outside people has been in touch. The most elaborate of these jargons, almost deserving to be called a language, was developed in northeastern Alaska and northwestern Canada between the Eskimos and the Tinneh or Athapascans. The jargon used in most of Alaska was started by the early whalers who worked on the basis of another jargon which had been developed by American whalers up around Baffin Island and Hudson Bay. As spoken today, this jargon consists of between three and five hundred Eskimo words, which are used uninflected and sometimes in very strange meanings. In this Alaska jargon there are a few words from the Chinook jargon of Washington State and British Columbia, introduced by gold miners. A number of the words are from a jargon developed between white and natives in the Hawaiian Islands and some are from pidgin Chinese. Danish, French, Spanish, and English are all represented by a few words.

Naturally it is impossible to express any but the simplest ideas in five or six hundred uninflected words, and this is no doubt the chief reason why so many white people in Alaska will tell you that the ideas of the Eskimos are very simple. They are in reality very complicated, although it is a complexity different from that of our mechanistic age and vocabulary.

Under primitive conditions Eskimos always shared their food, so that no one went hungry while others had plenty. They were all well-fed or hungry together. Unlike the Indians, Eskimos had no chiefs, no slaves and aristocrats; in fact, they had no caste. No one held office. No man could order another to do his bidding. Men of judgment and skill were looked up to and consulted, but because of their superior wisdom or talent, not because of rank. There was equality between men and women; a husband could not *order* his wife to do any-

78

thing, or vice versa. All common problems of these essentially gentle people were discussed amicably and often at great length. Their exuberant happiness seems to have been the result of good health and of a fortunately natural attitude toward life and death.

Relatively little of the old ways remain today except their remarkably cheerful spirit, and the fine quality of their relations with each other and the outside world. Their adaptability has made the bridge between their past life and the difficult new one that faces them, a short one. Most Eskimos who used to be protected by distance from the white man's ways, have been reached, in connection with the DEW Line, White Alice, and allied installations. Many have become excellent workers in the construction and maintenance of our various defense structures.

The best bush pilot I flew with in Alaska was an Eskimo working for Northern Consolidated. The mechanical skills reported by early explorers have made other Eskimos excellent mechanics, tractor drivers, carpenters, and radio operators. There are Eskimo plane dispatchers, nurses, soldiers, businessmen, hotel and store keepers, legislators and teachers. At the Arctic Research Laboratory at Point Barrow two Eskimos were working as expert laboratory technicians. The Director told me each was "worth two white men apiece." His Darwinian survival-of-the-fittest theory is that life in the Far North for many hundreds of years was so difficult for Eskimos that only the quick-witted, sharp-sighted hunter with good judgment and quick reflexes, managed to survive. The present-day Eskimos are his descendents.

In the first century of his contact with the white man, the arctic Eskimo, unlike his more southerly relatives, never stood in awe of western civilization. For in northernmost Eskimo territory the white man was uncomfortable, if not helpless, without Eskimo clothing, Eskimo guides, Eskimo dogs and sledges, and his food had to be shipped in from the outside. The Eskimo was, and felt himself to be, the superior man.

Today the picture has been reversed. Eskimo ideals have been largely exchanged for those of the white man. Although he is on the average quicker, more observant and more patient than the white man, the Eskimo no longer feels superior. Many are uncertain of just what their role should be in a hydrogen bomb age. Most feel certain that a white man's education will better equip them for a good life in a white man's world. Each year more Eskimos receive better schooling in Alaska. Another step in the direction of their new goal was taken in June, 1958, at the University of Alaska, when, among the graduates receiving degrees and commissions in the Air Force, for the first time in history, a full-blooded Eskimo received his lieutenant's bars.

Chapter Five

Life in a Northern Alaskan Village

Close to 64° north latitude at the head of Norton Sound, a typical coastal village faces Bering Sea. Seward to the southeast is a little less than five hundred miles away, Barrow to the northeast, a little more. This is not the biggest village in Alaska, nor yet the smallest; it is not the most civilized, nor the most primitive. Winters here are long and cold, but flower gardens blaze with color in summer and vegetables grow to great size. Nome, the nearest "city" is one hundred and fifty miles away but no road connects the two settlements.

This is an Alaskan village, one of many that leaped from the era of the dog sled to that of the airplane with no intervening stages. It is not unusual to find here an Eskimo dog sledger who is also an expert bush pilot but cannot drive an automobile. Sledges and planes are numerous and familiar, automobiles few and very new. The Eskimo population of about six hundred has now largely exchanged *kammiks* for shoepacks, reindeer skin clothing for blue jeans and zipper jackets, and Eskimo food delicacies like *akutok* for canned fruit salad.

Akutok, or Eskimo ice cream as it is sometimes called, is a party food not unlike our suet puddings, which the Eskimos at Unalakleet made from berries, seal oil, and reindeer suet, all beaten together until the mixture was the consistency of ice cream. Each year another bit of old Eskimo culture is left behind and more of the white man's speech, technology, medicine, and way of life acquired. Here people are now as familiar with hillbilly music, radar, and Air Force slang as with ancient sealing methods, the training of sled dogs, and the best places to fish for salmon in the nearby Unalakleet River. Our village is named Unalakleet too, pronounced Yóu-na-lak-léet, with the first and fourth syllables accented. On an average summer day at the Trading Post you might discover, in addition to Eskimo housewives, meteorologists, engineers, pilots, and workmen from nearby defense installations. Servicemen, too, come into town to buy Eskimo ivory carvings to send home to their families. Eskimo children romp and giggle. Whether school is in session or out, summer or winter, good weather or bad, the sound of laughter is never long absent in an Eskimo village, and Unalakleet is no exception.

Inland from a shelving sandy beach is a ridge on which the village houses are built. Back of the ridge is a strip of land running parallel to the beach which the river floods each spring. From here the land rises slowly and evenly to the Shaktoolik hills. North of the river these hills come down to the shore in high bluffs of sandstone.

Christianity has now reached the entire Eskimo world from Greenland through Canada to Alaska, except for the small group of Eskimos in northeastern Siberia. There Soviet Communism may be said to replace Christianity as a religion. Missionary work among the Eskimos started during the eighteenth century in Greenland and Labrador, and still continues. The sincere acceptance of Christianity by the Eskimos does not necessarily wipe out all memory and practices of their ancient religion. Among church-going Eskimo Christians it is not unusual to find traces of their ancient religious beliefs in the observance of certain hunting customs, or the naming of children.

There are almost as many denominations of Christianity in Alaska as in the world. Each Church sends out missions to different parts of the state and that denomination becomes the established religion. The Moravians, for instance, dominate the Kuskokwim area, the Episcopalians are at Point Hope and Fort Yukon, the Presbyterians at Point Barrow and so on. The Roman Catholics, Methodists, Greek Orthodox, Salvation Army, Assembly of God, Seventh Day Adventists, and many other sects are also represented. In the larger settlements there are sometimes rival missions, but in towns the size of Unalakleet one denomination usually prevails. Here the mission is a part of the Evangelical Covenant Church of America which has headquarters in Chicago. The active church members numbered about one hundred and fifty in 1958. On Sun-

The church at Unalakleet.

day mornings some two hundred, including many non-Eskimos, attend services. A handsome new church was completed in the spring of 1955 by local Eskimos working under the direction of a professional missionary builder, a practice common with other denominations too in Alaska.

The Church used to maintain an orphanage at Unalakleet, but in 1955 it was moved and a high school, for which there was greater need, started in its stead. The school has a staff of six, which includes the Reverend Maynard D. Londborg, who teaches science, mathematics, government and Bible classes, in addition to his duties as pastor. Mrs. Londborg is the school nurse and also teaches Bible, health and piano classes. Commercial courses, industrial arts, English, history, and home economics are taught, and in addition to all courses required by Alaska's Department of Education, many electives are also

School children at Unalakleet.

offered. The first graduation took place in May, 1958, with nine of the school's thirty-four students acquiring diplomas. In addition to town students, about ten young people come from neighboring villages and live in the school dormitory for the term.

In Eskimo villages considerably smaller than Unalakleet there is sometimes neither school nor schoolteacher. About two hundred children from such communities attend the Wrangell Boarding School maintained by the Alaska Native Service which teaches them through the eighth grade. The Native Service also administers the much larger Mount Edgecumbe Boarding School at Sitka. Here the buildings of the decommissioned Sitka Naval Air Station have been converted into one of the best equipped educational institutions in Alaska. More than seven hundred students, under the supervision of a large teaching staff, are taught through junior high school. Excellent vocational training is available as well. Mount Edgecumbe offers the only possibility of a high school education to most of the natives living in small villages where there are no grades beyond the eighth. Boys at Edgecumbe may learn boatbuilding, carpentry, plumbing, and about electricity and machines. Girls train as nurses, office workers, or learn the arts of homemaking.

It is difficult for an Eskimo child to leave the warmth and love that surrounds him in his family circle, to travel hundreds of miles to a strange school. There he finds teachers and innumerable classmates, but not a single familiar face. Affectionate parents find it equally hard to part with their youngsters. Both make what seems to them a great sacrifice to obtain an education which will better prepare the boy or girl for a good life in a white man's world. A world, incidentally, that young Eskimos embrace on the whole with the greatest interest and enthusiasm.

85

S E A

Here is

ALASKA

R A N G E

ON R.　Fort Yukon

ollege
Fairbanks

Tanana River

ALASKA

R A N G E

HIGHWAY

C A N A D A

A L A S K A

HUGACH

M T S

Valdez

Mt. St. Elias

Cordova

Skagway

Haines

Mendenhall Glacier

Juneau

Douglas

GULF

of

ALASKA

ALEXANDER

Sitka

ARCHIPELAGO

Wrangell

Ketchikan

Metlakatla

Annette

140°

50　　0　　　　100　　　　200

Scale in Miles

V. English

EUTIAN ISLANDS

ISLANDS OF
THE FOUR
MOUNTAINS

Umnak

Nikolski

T ISLANDS

ka

chitka I.

180°

ANDREANOF IS.

Atka I

0　　MILES　150

170°

Twice a year, in late May and early September, all the airlines of Alaska engage in a tremendous airlift as some nine hundred Indian, Eskimo and Aleut children are transported free from home to school, or school to home. Every civilian air carrier has a part in trying to deliver each child at his home on the same day as he left school. This is no easy task when you consider that a Point Barrow youngster must travel more than twelve hundred miles from Sitka to reach home. The school airlift is thought to be the largest civilian air movement ever staged in Alaska. Extra flights are scheduled, but vacant seats on regular passenger flights are also utilized by quick-to-smile Eskimo or Indian youngsters.

Alaska has two separate school systems. One is Federal, under the Bureau of Indian Affairs, with an enrollment of 4,500; the other is a formerly Territorial, but now State directed system. This is supported by Alaskan taxation, and has a much higher enrollment of 35,000. Private schools, mostly church-connected like Unalakleet's high school, account for only 4 per cent of Alaska's schools.

About half of the Eskimo and Indian children attend Federal schools and half State schools. Both types are attended by natives and white. There is no segregation. The Alaska Native Service, under the Federal system, operates over eighty day schools, mainly in isolated outlying districts. As the State system grows it is expected eventually that all schools will come under its supervision. This is practically the case now in southeastern Alaska.

There is an important difference in philosophy between Alaska Native Service and State schoolteachers. ANS teachers are civil servants and work for twelve months of the year, although they teach for only eight months. They assume certain social service duties, such as postmaster, or radio operator, and are usually important and influential figures in the community. State schoolteachers think this is a form of paternalism. They teach for nine months of the year and that is all they do. They offer no extracurricular social service work except as normal citizens of the community. Education in both rural and district schools of the State system is exactly the same. Lest you think that it lags behind our other states in quality, a recent survey has shown that in fundamental studies Alaskan schools rate 10 per cent higher scholastically than the United States schools south of the Canadian border!

Teachers in both school systems, and anthropologists too, agree that Eskimo and Indian children are as bright as any other children. But in Alaska they are handicapped in their learning by being taught from the same textbooks that are

Twice a year this Point Barrow boy may fly more than 1200 miles to his school in Sitka.

used in the other forty-eight states. Many of the ideas and examples contained in these otherwise excellent books are completely foreign to them. Subways, skyscrapers, superhighways, elevators, huge department stores—these are necessarily imaginary for most Eskimo children.

All classes in Alaska are conducted in English. If you can picture yourself knowing no Latin and attending first grade only to discover that your teacher speaks and understands only Latin, and that you can communicate with her in no other language, you will have an insight into how an Eskimo-speaking child feels on the first day of school. By now most Alaskan Eskimos have learned to speak some form of English and the language barrier is not as high as it was once. Unfortunately though, many Eskimos have learned English at the expense of forgetting their own wonderful language.

In Greenland where children are taught in the Eskimo language, a child learns far more quickly than his Alaskan cousins do. Almost immediately the Greenlanders begin to study a second language—Danish. As a result, all Greenlanders not only read and write Eskimo, but they write, illustrate, and print newspapers and books in Greenland in that language. They have translated the great world classics into their own tongue, and proudly developed a literary tradition, while preserving their ancient language. In Alaska, if an Eskimo wants to learn about the world, he can do so only in English, since almost nothing, with the exception of religious books, is published in his language. It is a pity that such a "marvelous tool of the intellect," as Eskimo has been referred to by one linguist, is destined to die out in Alaska.

More than thirty years ago missionaries and schoolteachers first planted small gardens in Unalakleet, so that they might have fresh vegetables for their personal use. In 1923, a Swedish missionary, the Reverend Ernest B. Larsson, interested the Eskimos in agriculture. He obtained the necessary seed and carefully instructed the people in planting and in cultivation methods, personally supervising most of the gardens the first year. He must have been proud when, three years later, the first commercial crop from local gardens was shipped out.

Potatoes were the main crop then, but cabbage, cauliflower, rutabagas, turnips, carrots, beets, parsnips, lettuce, celery, onions, rhubarb, peas, radishes, Swiss chard, and spinach were all grown successfully. Each year five or six thousand dollars' worth of produce was grown, and most of it shipped to nearby Nome. The surplus was stored in local cellars, cooled by natural permafrost, and saved for winter use.

An Eskimo woman prepares the vegetables she has grown in her garden.

The growing season at Unalakleet is short, if you reckon it by weeks, but longer if you count it by hours of sunshine. In June there is daylight for twenty-four hours, although the sun sets around 10:30 or 11:00 P.M. Local folk credit the great size and the goodness of their products to the long periods of sunlight. Twenty tons used to be an average potato crop. In 1957, Frank Ryan, the postmaster, raised 1,700 pounds of potatoes, just in his spare time. But the cultivation of vegetables, which once provided an important source of cash for the village, has dwindled considerably, because of high wages paid in defense construction. When an Eskimo can earn a minimum wage of $225.00 per week working on a White Alice or DEW Line station, he is not likely to spend much time cultivating a garden.

The Civil Aeronautics Administration, or CAA, is a Federal agency charged with collecting and dispensing weather information, handling flight plans, reporting on landing conditions, and controlling air-ground communication and air traffic throughout Alaska. They do all these things in Unalakleet, and also provide and maintain the town's two runways.

The CAA employed ten people from eight families there in 1958, including two natives. Regularly scheduled commercial airlines, flying in and out daily, use the CAA airfields, as do the military and semi-military aircraft used in building and maintaining the nearby White Alice and Aircraft Control and Warning radar site.

Wonderful fishing in the vicinity, and the easy air accessibility of Unalakleet, have resulted in the construction of an Air Force recreation center. Grayling, tomcod, and salmon abound in the local river, supplying some food and much pleasure to local and visiting anglers. Commercial fishing is still forbidden. A King Salmon Derby is now an annual event. The first prize in 1957 was won by a forty-six pounder!

What do people like the CAA men do with themselves at a place like Unalakleet when their work is done for the day? The most popular hobbies are photography, hunting, and amateur radio. Donn F. Baker, the station manager, and his wife Thelma are both ham radio fans and each maintains a separate station. Should you want to visit with them via the radio waves, Donn's number is KL7ASQ, Thelma's is KL7BEW.

In early 1958 a power plant was installed which provides electricity for the entire village. To those of us who unthinkingly flip switches on and off dozens of times a day, taking electricity for granted, it is hard to imagine what electric service means to a northern Eskimo village like Unalakleet when it first comes.

Eklutna's hydroelectric power station.

Remember that in winter there is no flowing water, as low temperatures gradually freeze the sources of summer supply. Water for drinking, cooking, for cleaning, for washing clothes and bathing, must all be melted in huge pots, from river ice. The ice must first be cut at some distance from the village and then brought to town by dog team, more recently by truck. You would be surprised at how much bulky ice it takes to melt enough water for a bath, how much fuel must be burned in the process, and how long it takes ice to be transformed from a solid to a liquid state.

Then, imagine the fire hazard presented in a dry temperature (and at low temperatures the air is always extremely dry) by the filling, cleaning, and lighting of kerosene lamps. The kindling and replenishing of oil stoves used for heating and cooking, and kept going at maximum capacity during the bitterly low midwinter temperatures, add to the danger. In this country, even more than in most rural places, a fire once started is unlikely to be quenched by man. It often wipes out an entire settlement. There are no conveniently placed hydrants to which fire hoses can be attached, and even if there were, the water would not flow at midwinter temperatures. A fire, however small, threatens every house in the village. Northerners have a constant fear of fire, and feel considerably safer where electricity is used.

Since World War II Unalakleet has changed from a fairly remote Eskimo village to which a few white man's ideas and techniques had penetrated, to an Eskimo village where white man's culture dominates and some few Eskimo customs remain.

Besides the White Alice station, the radar warning site, CAA installations, daily plane connections with other Alaskan towns, and the new high school, there is a Public Health nurse now who gives polio shots and administers TB chemotherapy. The presence of young military men and their recreation center is new. So are the tourists and the King Salmon Derby. Formerly, except for visiting scientists, and Coast Guard vessels stopping by in summer, there were few new faces to be seen in town. Now there are more than one can memorize.

The Trading Post, established in 1913, is still open. Glen and Lloyd Glancy own and operate it now. It is still the biggest, most important shopping center in town, but it is one of five, including an Alaska Native Store. The Post still has a lighterage business, for Unalakleet, like most coastal towns in northern Alaska, has no harbor. Cargo ships must anchor far offshore and all supplies are shifted to barges which haul them ashore. The Post no longer houses the radio station and post office; they have grown sufficiently to warrant buildings of their own. Instead, it now shelters a hotel and restaurant, the latter complete with juke box and ice cream machine. Above the restaurant there is a movie house seating one

Barge building at Unalakleet.

hundred and fifty. Three times a week movies are shown, double features on Saturday, and it is equipped with the latest Cinemascope machines.

Unalakleet has automobiles now. In 1957, when one of the government defense installations was completed, more than a dozen cars, mostly pickup trucks, were sold to the natives. The fact that no road connects Unalakleet with any other town matters not at all. The White Alice station is fourteen miles away, the Aircraft Control and Warning radar site, AC & W for short, about six miles off; otherwise all traffic is confined to Unalakleet. Having lots of cars and no place to go, except from one end of town to the other, is not an unusual situation in Alaska. It occurs even in some of the larger cities.

As always happens when something new comes in, something old goes out. Missing or fading from the local scene are the old houses which have been exchanged for log cabins and clapboard houses. Gone are the white whale hunts, in which the entire male population used to take part, and which were always followed by *maktak* feasts and celebrations. Few now are the summer migrations of families up river to catch their winter's fish supply. Fewer seals are hunted, there is less sharing of food, which always used to accompany hunting success. Now there are bigger and better trading posts offering innumerable items never seen before in the way of food, tools, and gadgets, all intriguing, all expensive, and all wanted by the modern Eskimo. Perhaps one of the most striking differences is the almost total absence of the once familiar and numerous reindeer herds in the vicinity.

Back in the years between 1892 and 1902, under the leadership of the noted educator, Dr. Sheldon Jackson, the United States Government imported 1,280 reindeer from Siberia with a view to supplementing the dwindling animal life on which the Eskimo depended. If protected, reindeer will double in numbers every three years, and the original herd increased eventually to an estimated half million. In 1937, after passage of an act by Congress, the government purchased all herds owned by whites for redistribution among the natives.

About two hundred animals were assigned to a family in many Eskimo villages, including Unalakleet. Eskimos, however, are not by nature or tradition herders, and when new and more interesting methods of earning a living appeared on the horizon, herding declined. The neglected tame deer ran off and joined the caribou herds. Once a goodly portion of the food consumed in town was reindeer meat; once the deerskins were sewn into handsome, light-weight but extremely warm winter clothing. This is no longer true today.

To the old-timer, nothing brings home the irony of the phrase "the blessings of civilization" more than the appearance of a dentist in an Eskimo community. Fifty or seventy-five years ago he could not have earned a living in Unalakleet because then every Eskimo had perfect teeth.

One of the marvels reported by early explorers was the way Eskimos could use their mouths as we use a vise or a claw hammer, as an extra tool. The strength of jaw and teeth was startling to us, as for instance their ability to pull a nail from a board with their teeth. In those days every tooth in every Eskimo head was sound. Sometimes the teeth were worn down to the gums with use, and occasionally even broken, but even then they never decayed. Nutritionists and anthropologists believe that where you find decayed teeth you have people who eat carbohydrates. When the white man introduced his food to the Eskimos—flour, sugar, hard bread, and molasses—he introduced tooth decay as well.

Around 1910 it was common in Alaska to meet people who could remember when they first heard of tooth decay and toothache. After shifting from the wholesome primitive diet to a white man's diet, it takes between four and ten years for the first cavities to appear. The teachers at Unalakleet instruct their pupils in tooth brushing and dental hygiene; but few of them mention that before Eskimos learned to brush their teeth they had *no* cavities; while now they have both toothache and cavities. The teeth of Eskimo villagers are just as bad as ours now; it is not uncommon, alas, to see young Eskimos in their thirties with complete dentures.

One of Unalakleet's personality changes is in the type of house now used by the villagers. The traditional Eskimo thick-walled earth house used to be typical. With driftwood or whale-bone rafters, it was so cold-proof that a small amount of blubber burning in a moon-shaped lamp kept it warm enough for families to sit around in the evenings either stripped to the waist or lightly clad. Children ran about naked as they did in ancient times.

Contrary to a surprisingly strong popular belief, Alaskans *never* used the snow house as a dwelling, even before the coming of the white man. The dome-shaped house built of wind-packed snow blocks, and held in place by ingenious engineering and gravity, was confined to an area in central arctic Canada, east of the Mackenzie River. Use of the snow house extended eastward from there as far as one section of northwestern Greenland where a small group known as the Polar Eskimos used it. But they were the only Greenlanders who did. South of the Polar Eskimos, only the earth, and the earth and stone house, was used. No Asiatic Eskimos ever used the snow dome structure either.

A completely mistaken but still popular belief is that "all Eskimos live in igloos, and igloos are houses made of ice blocks." The Eskimo word *igloo*, better spelled *iglu*, is a general term meaning a temporary or permanent shelter for man or beast.

Railway stations, cathedrals, tents, school houses, and family dwellings are all igloos. A snow house is an igloo, too; but its own special name in the Mackenzie dialect is *apudyak*, from *apun*, the name for snow that is lying on the ground, as if ready to be cut into snow blocks for house building. In a few areas white men have told the natives that the word igloo should be reserved for a snow house, and some Eskimos now use it so.

A satisfactory snow house cannot be made of ice. Ice is a good conductor of temperature and would quickly transmit the outside chill indoors. Snow on the other hand is a poor conductor, which means it is an excellent insulator, thanks to the numerous air spaces captured within it. It can be cut in suitable blocks, is light to handle, easy to shave and carve so that blocks fit neatly and lean at the proper angle. The colder the outdoor temperature, the warmer the inside of a snow house may be safely heated. Experienced travelers who have tried both tents and snow houses in winter camping, invariably prefer the snow house as being more comfortable.

Alaskan Eskimos, as said, never used the snow houses for winter dwellings, as their neighbors to the east did. Some Alaskans knew of the existence of snow houses, a few having learned the skill from explorers or Canadian Eskimos, and then used them as traveling camps. Today all Alaskan Eskimos know about them, and most know how to build a good one. Many have learned through serving in the National Guard, or through reading books like my husband's *Arctic Manual*, which gives precise instructions and helpful drawings. And, of course, now they have all seen these snow houses in the movies.

The commonest type of house being built in Alaska, whether among whites or Eskimos, is a wooden house, built usually of imported lumber. Compared to an earth house, it is expensive, drafty, and spendthrift of fuel, but it is *fashionable* and we all know how women, or for that matter men too, will suffer in the name of fashion.

A single earth house remains in Unalakleet, and it is not a proper old-fashioned earth-walled house, but a kind of earth-banked log cabin. This is a transition style of architecture, a

In wintertime huge snowdrifts form wherever a house or object faces the wind. Where there is no obstruction the wind swept ground is almost bare.

An earth-roofed cache or storehouse built high out of reach of dogs.

An Eskimo boy comes down the ladder from the cache.

combination of the white man's log cabin, with the Eskimo idea of using earth for insulation. Fortunately those of us who have never seen any kind of earth house, or seen how life was lived in one, may still discover all about it. Fred and Sara Machetanz have captured it for us in words, drawings, and on film.

Fred and Sara are an Alaskan couple. He is an artist, writer, photographer, and lecturer, whose uncle, Charlie Traeger, founded the Trading Post at Unalakleet. A typical sourdough, Traeger was lured north by the Gold Rush and like many before and after him, fell in love with the country. He stayed and settled in Unalakleet to become one of the most influential members of the community. Fred came to visit him for a summer, was "adopted" by the village, and stayed for two years. When he left, his notebooks were crammed with sketches and detailed notes of Unalakleet's Eskimo way of life. His notes were transformed into several books for children.

Sara and Fred Machetanz at work on their log cabin in the Matanuska Valley.

In 1947 Fred married Sara in the old mission. Uncle Charlie gave them a gala wedding reception, attended by the entire village. Thereafter Sara took over the writing, freeing Fred to cultivate a new talent, movie-making.

Together they produced four more books and in 1954-55 spent a year and a half in and around Unalakleet, making a film about sled dogs for Walt Disney. While living in the last of the earth houses, they raised a team of seven sled pups, all of whom played important roles in the film. The Machetanzes now spend half of every year lecturing and showing their colored films of the North. The other half is spent traveling in Alaska with the Matanuska Valley as their home base. They have built a log cabin on a high hill in that fertile area outside of Palmer.

Unalakleet adopted the Machetanzes and they returned the compliment by capturing the town, the people, and a vanishing way of life on canvas, paper, and film.

The finished house where Sara writes books about Alaska and Fred illustrates them.

Chapter Six

Interesting Islands

LOOKING INTO TOMORROW

Up North where Bering Sea meets the Arctic Sea and Siberia and Alaska seem to be reaching out to join hands, are two little islands. These are the rocky Diomedes. Standing on Little Diomede you can see across to another hemisphere, into another day of the week! For Little Diomede is part of Alaska in the Western Hemisphere, while Big Diomede belongs to the Soviet Union in the Eastern Hemisphere. Only a narrow strait separates the islands but through this strait runs the International Date Line, on the other side of which is a new day. When it is Monday in Alaska on Little Diomede, it is Tuesday in Siberia on Big Diomede. You can look into tomorrow from Little Diomede or, if you are standing on the larger island, you can peer into yesterday.

The Eskimos who live on both islands are interrelated and, with little thought of Date Lines and International Boundaries, used to visit back and forth by boat in summer, or afoot in

winter when the strait was frozen over. This was a privilege reserved for Eskimos only, and during World War II this infor-
mal and friendly interchange ended. After the war, in 1948,
when eighteen Little Diomeders thought it time to resume the
old ways, they went across to the bigger island to visit and
trade as they had often done in prewar times. They were ar-
rested by Soviet officers, imprisoned, but eventually released.

*The cobbled street
village on Little
Diomede is within
sight of Asia.*

Now it doesn't matter whether you are Eskimo or white, it is inadvisable to set foot on Big Diomede. There are rumors, however, that in midwinter Eskimos from both islands sometimes meet and visit in the middle of the frozen strait.

Vitus Bering was a Dane who began his long service in the Russian Imperial Navy at the age of twenty-three. Peter the Great placed him at the head of an expedition charged with

determining whether or not the continents of Asia and America were connected. In 1725 he embarked on what has been called one of the most remarkable undertakings in the history of exploration and science, really a series of expeditions, lasting many years and involving hundreds of men. On August 16, 1728, St. Diomede's day, he sighted two islands and named them after the saint. A heavy curtain of fog prevented Bering from seeing what he had traveled so far to discover, the coast of America, and he turned back soon afterward. What a trick of fate was this! Had the weather been good he would have returned to St. Petersburg triumphant. Instead, his first three years of intense labor were considered wasted and the opening expedition of the series counted a failure.

It is a common belief that once there was a land bridge between Alaska and Siberia by which the animals of North America and Asia migrated back and forth. The Diomedes, placed where the distance between the two continents is smallest, only fifty-six miles, were probably part of this bridge. Some believe that twenty, thirty, or forty thousand years ago, when man first arrived in America from Asia, he was able to walk across Bering Strait on an ice bridge that was part of the glacial age. Others think a land bridge existed then. More likely the first human discoverers of America came in skin boats similar to the Eskimo umiak, which we know is capable of long sea voyages and carrying as many as sixty or more people. Neither of the Diomedes has a harbor, but that would not have mattered, for skin boats of that day would have been as easy to haul up on a rocky shore as the boats the islanders use today.

The design of an umiak is considered an ancient one, and is thought to have changed very little. Umiaks in use on the Diomedes today have the same sleek lines of their ancestors, but ribs instead of being made of driftwood, laboriously spliced, are now of imported hardwood and steam bent. Now too, likely as not, there will be an outboard motor attached to the stern.

Seal oil is still used for heating and cooking on Little Diomede Island, but it is burned in an enamel pan instead of a soapstone lamp as formerly, and the wick will be made of canvas instead of pussy willow fuzz or moss. Where hunting large game animals is still the chief means of support, fur clothing will be found too, for it is lighter, more comfortable, and more effective against the cold than white man's dress. But the furs will be supplemented by cotton dresses worn indoors by the women and cotton parkas worn over the furs to keep them dry. A common sight throughout Eskimo villages in Alaska now is a mixture of the two types of clothing.

Both of the treeless Diomedes rise from beachless shores, with almost perpendicular sides. On the smaller island the houses of Ignaluk, the only settlement, are perched in terraces along the steep sides of the island. In 1950, 103 people lived in the village, which at first glance resembles a medieval town. It has streets paved with cobblestones, complete with gutters draining the water. Unlike most primitive Eskimo dwellings, the Diomede houses are in the main built of rocks held together with clay. Bits of driftwood are utilized whenever they can be found, supplemented in recent years by imported timber. Roofs were formerly of walrus skin, but shingled roofs are not uncommon now.

The deep surrounding waters supply walrus, whale and seal, still the mainstay of the Diomede diet. A few bears and foxes are taken too, but all are supplemented by store-bought canned milk, tea, sugar, flour, and cigarettes.

Not long ago the remote Diomede Islanders and their way of life were typical of Alaska's Eskimos. Today they represent the exception rather than the rule.

HERE IS ALASKA

MISTY HOME OF THE FUR SEALS

Two hundred and fourteen miles north of the nearest land are five islands that make up the Pribilof group, also known as the Seal Islands. They are St. Paul, St. George and three much smaller uninhabited islands, Otter, Walrus, and Sealion Rock. The seals arriving here each year are probably the only aquatic animals in the world that have the honor of being escorted to their summer home by the U.S. Coast Guard, which protects them from illegal hunters at sea.

The islands are named after their Russian discoverer, Gavriil Pribilof. In 1786, while sailing among the Aleutians, he noticed the migrating seals and decided to try and follow them

Group of fur seals, Pribilof Islands.

to their breeding grounds, the location of which had long been a tantalizing mystery. He sailed northward and by chance took an almost direct route to the rookeries. He landed on June 12 and named the new island St. George, after his ship. So foggy is this area that it was a year before St. Paul, the larger island, was sighted, although it is only forty miles away.

Since then the misty Pribilofs have become famous as the largest fur seal rookery in the world. The precipitous islands are volcanic in origin and for nine days out of ten in summer are enveloped in fog. Here there are only two seasons, foggy wet summer and dry, windy winter. The damp summer climate and the numerous sheltered rocky areas are so perfectly adapted, however, to the needs of the breeding fur seal that 80 per cent of the world's fur seal population comes here to have its young. The Pribilof seal differs from fur seals living in the Southern Hemisphere, and is unlike the much more widely distributed, smaller, hair seal. The latter animal, in contrast to the silky, luxurious coat of the fur seal, has a short, stiff-haired pelt, and is hunted for food and fuel by Eskimos from Siberia all the way to Greenland.

Neither of the two larger Pribilofs has a harbor, and navigation is dangerous. The group lies near the southern limit of scattered ice in Bering Sea and detached pieces of arctic pack may be seen bobbing offshore between February and May. The steep coasts also provide excellent seasonal housing for a hundred species of bird life including auklets, cormorants, gulls, murres, kittiwakes and sea parrots.

Once Pribilof discovered the breeding grounds of the fur seal, wholesale slaughter followed. It has been estimated that between 1799 and 1834 two million animals were killed. From 1835 until the Alaska Purchase, it was forbidden to kill female seals, with a hope of preserving the diminishing herds.

Later, when the route of the annual migration was discovered, came pelagic sealing, or the taking of seals at sea. Schooners would follow the herds from the Oregon coast to the Seal Islands, killing as they sailed. They would lie off the islands waiting for the mothers as they went to sea to secure food for their young. This was double murder. If a mother didn't return her baby died of starvation, since a seal will nurse no pup but her own. In an effort to stop this wanton slaughter the United States called conferences and passed laws, but to no avail. These laws drove the sealers to register under foreign flags, and they managed to get many seals despite revenue cutters patrolling the sea.

By 1910 it was estimated that indiscriminate hunting had reduced the fur seal population from three million to one hundred and twenty-five thousand. In that year our government took charge of the rookeries and finally negotiated a treaty with Great Britain, Japan, and Russia, by which pelagic sealing was outlawed. Since then, through care and scientific management the herd has increased and is now estimated at a fairly constant one and a half million. Each year a small percentage of young males are killed for their pelts, and in 1956, for the first time in many years, because of too great an increase, some females were taken. Between 1940 and 1956 the average annual take was about sixty-five thousand. The skins are sold at fur auctions and then made up into sealskin coats. To date the sale of sealskins has brought the government more than twice the purchase price of Alaska! In 1957 the surplus animals taken were valued at more than five million dollars.

In 1940 Japan denounced the fur seal treaty and proclaimed that her sealers would take animals wherever and whenever they could. Following the war, in 1957, an interim North Pacific fur seal convention was concluded by Canada,

Japan, the Soviet Union, and the United States. It is similar in form to the earlier one which provides that Canada and Japan shall receive 15 per cent of the sealskins taken commercially by both the United States and the U.S.S.R.

Names given to members of a fur seal family are curious. The mature male is called a "bull," his wife a "cow," and their youngsters are "pups." A bull and his wives constitute a "harem" and a congregation of harems is a "rookery." The three-year-old males are called "bachelors" and they are the ones that are killed each year.

The fur seals are first cousins to the sea lion. They live from twelve to fifteen years and the male usually weighs four to six times as much as the female. After she is three years old the cow gives birth to one pup annually, soon after her arrival on the island. After the pup is weaned the mother goes to sea in search of food for her offspring and may travel a great distance, remaining away for days. On her return, by a secret process known only to mother seals, she can always spot her own child among the thousands of pups waiting on the beach.

Although the Pribilofs are treeless, they are covered in summertime with deep green and yellow-green vegetation. Many a visitor has been pleasantly surprised when the fog lifted to disclose the islands, bright with the color of flowering plants, luxuriant grasses and moss.

There are Aleut villages on St. Paul and St. George. It was from these settlements, as well as the Aleutian Islands, that puzzled and dismayed natives were evacuated to Admiralty Island during World War II. They have since returned. Most of them are engaged in the fur seal industry, under the supervision of the U. S. Fish and Wildlife Service.

MUSK OXEN AND REINDEER

In clear weather Nunivak Island, the second largest in Bering Sea, is visible in all directions for about thirty miles. Because it is surrounded by shoals which make boat approaches extremely dangerous, explorers and traders alike gave it a wide berth for many years. This circumstance permitted Nunivak's Eskimos to retain their ancient ways far longer than their mainland cousins. As late as 1926 Nunivak Islanders still wore bead and walrus ivory labrets, or lip ornaments, discarded long before by other western Eskimos. They still adhered religiously to elaborate ceremonies relating to seal hunting and social life in general. Then as now, walrus, seal, and fish were plentiful round the Island and the Nunivakers were prosperous.

Nunivak Island children. In the background is the daughter of the reindeer project manager.

Although the shift from old to new ways came late to the island, which lies off Alaska's western shore about midway between the Aleutians and Seward Peninsula, it was inevitable. With the intrusion of a new culture came the missionary, the schoolteacher, and eventually the bush pilot and his plane load of parcels from mail-order houses. To the Nunivak Eskimos, the change brought not only a new way of life but also two new animals for their island.

More than twenty years ago, in 1935 and 1936, thirty-one musk oxen, originally imported from Greenland, were moved from the mainland to Nunivak, which is a National Wildlife Refuge. These strange, prehistoric-looking beasts formerly roamed throughout the northern part of North America as far south as Kentucky. In mainland Alaska, probably the last native musk ox was killed south of Point Barrow around the 1870's. The tough, sturdy animals are perfectly adapted to arctic life, and defend themselves easily against all northern predatory animals except the grizzly bear. Bears were the reason for moving them to Nunivak, where there are neither bears nor wolves. Musk ox do not fear wolves, for wolves will not attack them unless they come upon a lone old animal or a lost calf.

Contrary to their reputation, musk oxen are seldom aggressors. When alarmed they usually run to the top of the nearest knoll, making a defensive formation with big animals on the outside and calves in the center. They charge singly, usually, each one making a short powerful rush of from ten to fifteen yards, then whirling, running back to the herd, facing about and backing into line. Their reported ferocity is largely imagined. Several polar expeditions have reported musk ox calves that domesticated themselves and became camp pets. More recently John Teal transferred seven calves from the

Canadian Arctic to his Vermont hill farm and has found them to be intelligent, gentle and easily domesticated.

The body of a musk ox is covered with long straggling stiff black hair, similar in texture to a horse's mane. In the roots of this hair grows a soft downy wool which is shed every spring, while the long guard hairs remain permanently. Short-legged and thick-bodied as they are, during the shedding season in April or May, their legs are often invisible, so long is the soft wool coat. The shedding wool drags in long tags after the animals and wisps may be picked up from the ground and bushes. The Eskimos call the musk ox *umingmak*, the bearded one.

A musk ox.

It is amusing to read again and again in various supposedly scientific books that a strong odor of musk surrounds the musk ox and pervades their meat. My explorer husband, who lived largely by hunting when he was in the Arctic, and who had innumerable meals of musk ox, reports that the meat is indistinguishable from beef, and has no trace whatever of musk odor. This is confirmed by other explorers, but somehow the old legend persists. It doubtless goes back to Elizabethan times when musk was a precious commodity, like gold, jewels, or spices, and the name represents a bit of wishful thinking on the part of some early explorer.

The milk of the musk ox is rich and creamy, but the wool is by far the most valuable part of the beast. The fuzzy stuff they shed each year is about half the weight of cashmere, lighter, finer, longer-fibered, and softer. It will not shrink even when washed with hot water and soap. Thus on Nunivak Island the 182 animals forming the herd (in 1958) are Alaska's only source of what is probably the world's most prized luxury wool. Actually, musk-ox wool is a misnomer; the undercoat of the animal is technically a hair, like camel's hair, cashmere, or vicuna.

Nunivak's other new animal is the reindeer, our name for a wild caribou when it is domesticated. Originally imported from Siberia into Alaska during the nineteenth century to supplement the native's dwindling supply of food, the dark brown, sometimes spotted, animals increased rapidly until at their peak they numbered almost half a million. Through neglect and ignorance they were almost wiped out during the late forties, but at last are increasing again, at least on Nunivak Island. In a few cases reindeer were placed on islands that had no wolves, their chief enemy, and permitted to run freely. They increased in number sufficiently to tax the grazing facilities of the islands, posing a threat of overgrazing and eventual starvation. Reindeer "moss," properly a lichen, is their main food, but it is an extremely slow growing plant, requiring many years to renew itself.

The islands where this condition prevailed were St. Matthew, Umnak, Atka and Nunivak. On Nunivak the problem was solved by the erection of a modern butchering, cold storage, and freezing plant to handle the surplus. Each year about three thousand animals are slaughtered, and their excellent meat sold commercially throughout the Kuskokwim valley area and Nome. About one-third of the meat is eaten on Nunivak and used to supplement the native diet in schools and hospitals run by the Alaska Native Service, which supervises the reindeer project. In 1956 the value of meat and skins sold was $140,000. This successful project, entirely self-supporting, gives useful employment to most of the male members of the island population, which numbers about three hundred in all.

In late summer every able-bodied man on the island takes part in the annual roundup. The reindeer are permitted to wander freely throughout the island all year. Only at butchering time are they herded and suitable animals picked for slaughtering. A walking fence is the first step in the roundup. The herders scatter and then slowly close in, driving the deer ahead of them. As they meet, each takes hold of a long piece of burlap, six or seven yards in length, crowding the animals in the direction of permanent wooden fences and v-shaped corrals, which lead into narrower inner corrals. Reindeer are sensitive and if startled tend to stampede, milling round and round in clockwise, tight-packed formation. All dogs in the neighborhood are tethered and kept out of sight at this time for they resemble wolves sufficiently to frighten the reindeer, and might start them running.

Eskimo women skin the animals. Flesh and fat are scraped from the skins, which are then hung up outdoors to be dried by wind and sun. Although there is a good market for reindeer horn needed by cutlery manufacturers, the horns are discarded, for Nunivak is so remote, transportation costs make it uneconomical to ship them.

Baling reindeer skins on Nunivak.

Despite the fashionable invasion of white man's food, thinking, and technology, there are some areas where Eskimo craft is still preserved because it surpasses anything the white man can devise. The skin boat is a good example. Wooden boats are in use on the island, to be sure, but for gliding swiftly and silently through ice-choked waters in search of seal or other game, the light, slender kayak is still supreme. Kayaks from the Nunivak area may be distinguished from others by the round holes in their prows which are useful as well as decorative. Umiaks, too, still compete successfully with wooden boats on Nunivak, because they are lighter and have a greater carrying capacity for their size. As mentioned before, they require extra care—the skin cover must be dried out between voyages to prevent rotting—but then they never require scraping and painting as wooden boats do.

At Mekoryuk, the main settlement on Nunivak, there is a native co-operative store where imported foodstuffs, hardware, and clothing are exchanged for money or ivory and wood carvings. The island is famous for its beautiful ceremonial masks depicting bird or animal images, which may be seen decorating the walls of Alaskan homes as well as museums throughout the world. On Nunivak the Swedish Covenant Church forbids the use of the handsome dance masks—indeed, forbids dancing. But the masks are still fashioned with native taste and skill and sold to visitors or to the Native Arts and Crafts Service which distributes them to gift shops throughout Alaska.

Like all modern Alaskan Eskimos, however remote from the centers of civilization their homes may be, male Nunivak Islanders of appropriate age now serve in the National Guard and go to training encampments on the mainland regularly, usually to Fort Richardson.

Although Nunivak Eskimos were later than most to welcome the white man and his ways, the completion of a large landing field on the island closes forever both symbolically and actually the gap which formerly separated island and mainland. Regular commercial flights, whatever the weather, will now replace sporadic visits of the bush pilot, and tourists, eager to see a musk ox or a reindeer roundup, will be arriving on Nunivak to inaugurate a new era.

ISLANDS OF THE SMOKY SEA

The treeless Aleutian Islands are the tops of a partially submerged mountain range which once linked Asia and America. Forming a continuation of the Alaska Range, they curve westward in a great arc to separate Bering Sea on the north from the Pacific Ocean to the south. From Alaska Peninsula to the outermost end of the chain almost eighty volcanoes have been counted, more than half of which have been active in historic times. Some parts of the volcanic rock are thought to be fifty million years old.

A surprising number of people think of these islands as arctic, but actually they lie between eight hundred and one thousand miles south of the Arctic Circle, in the latitude of England and northern France. In addition to innumerable islets and rocks, they consist of fourteen large and about fifty-five small, mountainous islands. The five main groups are the Fox Islands, closest to the mainland, the Islands of the Four Mountains, the Andreanofs, the Rat Islands, and the Near Islands named for their nearness to Kamchatka but farthest from the rest of Alaska.

The Aleutians are among the foggiest places in the world. When cold air meets warm air, the mingling produces fog.

At the Aleutian Islands the icy waters of Bering Sea sideswipe the warm Japan Current of the north Pacific Ocean. Result— what aviators call "pea soup" fog.

There are said to be only two seasons here, a rainy, foggy, cool summer and a comparatively mild, somewhat clearer winter. The thermometer never drops as low as zero, but cold, wet winds of high velocity blow across from Siberia to combine with warm air masses from the south. They produce rain, fog, mist, and snow. Good weather is rare and brief, shifting swiftly as the winds change. "Uncertain" is a word often used to describe Aleutian weather; "terrible" is probably the adjective *most* used.

"Williwaw" ("woolie" to the Yankee whalers of old) is a term familiar to all Aleutian Islanders but known too along other Alaskan coasts. It is a violent puff of wind that sweeps down suddenly with great force from a mountain slope. Because they come without warning and successive gusts change direction unexpectedly, williwaws are dangerous to vessels at sea or in harbor. A boat will toss wildly and is likely to break out her anchor or to capsize. A man cannot stand against a strong williwaw, and sailors, particularly those on small sailboats, have a healthy terror of them.

Williwaws, fog, and sudden storms have been responsible for some of the nicknames applied to the Aleutians. Birthplace of the Winds, Islands of the Smoky Sea, and Cradle of the Storms are among the more romantic ones. During World War II many soldiers stationed there invented new ones, few of them romantic and most of them not even polite. A rueful joke that made the rounds was "if the Japanese capture the Aleutians, it will serve them right." The men who had to fly bombing and scouting missions from Aleutian bases had cause for fear and complaint—fog, as well as Japanese gunfire, took so many of their young lives.

The innumerable passes between islands have strong and treacherous tidal currents. Contrary to popular belief, these channels are ice-free throughout the year. Sea ice never forms in the Aleutians except on the inner bays. The ocean is equally free of ice north and south of the chain. If you spent ten years atop the highest of the Aleutians with a telescope looking north into Bering Sea you would never see a cake of ice. It is only when you travel eastward toward Bristol Bay that floes begin to appear in the north.

The mild, highly intelligent Aleuts who inhabit these islands are of the same racial stock as the Eskimos. Although their languages are closely related in structure and basic vocabulary, they differ enough so they cannot understand one another. Like all other Eskimo-speaking peoples, the Aleut is of medium size, with short legs, large head and face, Mongoloid eyes, straight black hair and a scanty beard. They probably came to the islands from the mainland of Alaska in two separate migration waves. We think the first was more than four thousand years ago, the second within the last thousand years. It is thought that in their heyday they may have numbered twenty thousand—a far larger number than any neighboring Alaskan areas could support. But the riches of the surrounding sea were plentiful in sea lions, seals, and whales. Salmon and fowl were available, too; and, of great importance, ample supplies of driftwood for boat, tool, and weapon building. Aleut culture successfully aimed at developing self-sufficient individuals in a co-operative community. According to William Laughlin, only some twelve hundred genuine Aleuts survive today, less than one-sixteenth of their estimated original numbers. Over half of them live outside of the Aleutian Islands now, chiefly in the Pribilofs and on the Soviet Komandorski Islands. Alaska's 1950 census lists four thousand Aleuts, but this figure includes all native peoples living in the Aleutian area. To further confuse the picture, some Eskimos call themselves Aleuts and some Aleuts call themselves Eskimos.

The Aleut decline began soon after the Russians found the islands in 1741. Traders followed the explorers and were greeted hospitably by the friendly Aleuts. It is one of the darkest stories of European relations to "natives" that the Russians returned kindnesses with cruelties, thefts, and brutal killings, virtually enslaving the entire population. Aleuts were forced to spend their time hunting the fabulous sea otter, and of course to turn over the skins to the local representative of the Russian America Company. Both the Aleut and the sea otter decreased rapidly thereafter. Umnak Island, which once sheltered twenty-two villages and two thousand people, had by 1950 a single village, Nikolski, with a total of only fifty-nine inhabitants.

The sea otter, with perhaps the most precious of all furs, played an important role in early Alaskan history. Single otter skins have brought $1,500.00 in the memory of men still living. Four times heavier than the land otter, the sea otter is about four feet long, and may weigh anywhere from thirty to ninety pounds. They were practically exterminated during the eighteenth and nineteenth centuries by Russian fur hunters, or *promyshlenniki*.

It all started when the members of Vitus Bering's last expedition, sick and dying of scurvy, were shipwrecked on Bering Island. Here they found sea otters in abundance. The fresh meat cured their disease and gave them strength to build from the wreckage of their vessel a tiny namesake, the *St.*

An Aleut housewife blowing air through washed seal intestine. It will be stretched, dried and eventually made into waterproof coat.

Peter. Its limited cargo space was filled with fresh meat for the voyage back to Siberia, and into the remaining spaces the crew stuffed as many otter skins as they could. When they arrived in Petropavlovsk in 1742 they found the skins fetched enormous prices. This instantly inspired Siberian hunters to extend their hunting operations across Bering Strait to Alaskan waters.

So successful and greedy were the hunters that by the turn of this century the sea otter was thought to be extinct. Around 1910 the United States Government forbade the taking or sale of these animals, imposing heavy fines for the mere possession of a skin. Slowly a tiny remnant of the once huge herd began to increase.

In 1939 on Amchitka Island, largest of the Rat Island group, an interesting experiment in animal conservation began. As the "pods," or colonies, of sea otters grew, surplus animals were transplanted to other suitable islands to further increase their number. In 1957 success could be inferred from a Department of the Interior statement announcing that the newest count showed a far higher population than had been supposed. It was thought there might be as many as twenty thousand sea otter now swimming in Aleutian and Northwest Coast waters. The survival of the species now seems certain.

One sea otter herd numbering five hundred was assured of a permanent, private home when Simeonof Island, the most southeasterly of the Shumagin group off Alaska Peninsula, was declared a wildlife refuge in 1958. The luxuriant growth of seaweed here, the chief food of the protected otter, makes it an ideal sanctuary.

While the Russian role in the Aleutians was generally a grisly one, an exception to the rule can be found in the life of Father Ivan Veniaminov. He was not the first Russian missionary of Greek Orthodox faith in the Aleutians, but he was the first to master the difficult Aleut language and to interest himself in Aleut culture and welfare. In a native skin kayak, he paddled from island to island questioning people about their traditions and customs. For a decade following 1824 he lived in Unalaska, preaching and teaching, but also learning. Adapting the old Russian Cyrillic alphabet for the purpose, he created an Aleut alphabet which greatly aided the people in preserving their wonderfully complicated ancient language. Veniaminov opened a school where he taught Aleut children to read and write. He translated the Catechism and the Gospel of St. Matthew into Aleut and wrote an Aleut grammar.

An Aleut wedding in the Russian Orthodox Church. Crowns symbolizing holiness of marriage, must not rest on heads.

His painstaking writings still prove to be excellent source material for anthropologists and linguists. Under the name of Innocent, Father Veniaminov finally achieved the highest office of his church when he became Metropolitan of Moscow.

Many Russian traders settled in the Aleutians, marrying native girls. Modern Aleuts have a large measure of Russian blood; almost all have Russian names. Their church remains to this day the Russian Catholic, or Greek Orthodox Church.

When the numerous Russian massacres of the Aleuts finally came to a halt, white man's diseases, especially tuberculosis, became the killer. On their own diet the Aleuts were a healthy people and, as with the Eskimos, tooth decay was unknown among them. In adopting our ways, they also adopted our foods to the detriment of their health. The Alaska Department of Health now has a "floating health center," a ship named *Hygiene* which heads north in June to the isolated communities along the Alaska Peninsula and the Aleutian Islands in a worthy attempt to improve their failing health. But it is too late for most Aleuts.

A thrill of horror swept Alaska and the United States when, six months after Pearl Harbor, in June, 1942, the battleground of World War II shifted from far places to North America itself. The Japanese bombed Atka and Dutch Harbor. The following day they occupied Attu, the outermost Aleutian Island, killed the schoolteacher who was trying to send out news of the invasion, and took prisoner his wife and every other resident of the island. They were taken to Japan and interned in prisoner of war camps, where many of them died. Kiska Island was occupied, too.

Shortly afterward everyone living in the Aleutians was evacuated to the mainland. Forced to leave behind all they owned, the Aleuts were taken to evacuation camps in southeastern Alaska where many of them, for the first time in their lives, saw trees. Indeed, the heavily forested area in which they found themselves filled them with uneasy fear and a homesickness for their own familiar treeless landscape. Many went to work in salmon canneries, working side by side with their traditional enemies, the Indians.

At the war's end in 1945, they were permitted to return to their homes—all, that is, except the Attuans. Attu, one of the Near Islands, fourteen hundred miles west of Anchorage, is a lonely, isolated spot, difficult to defend. Its buildings had all been demolished in the war. Although the Attuans were eager to go home, the government decided their island should not be reoccupied and that Attuans should live on Atka Island, where there was a settlement closer to the mainland and easier to defend. So now Atka, some five hundred miles east of Attu, about midway in the chain, has the honor of being the most westerly community in North America—much more westerly than the Hawaiian Islands. The island is rugged and volcanic, and smoke still issues occasionally from its northern end. There is a Russian Orthodox Church and also a government schoolhouse at the settlement, which numbers less than seventy five.

In summertime, most able-bodied men on Atka leave the village for the Pribilof Islands where they work for the government in the fur seal rookeries. Their summer earnings are the sole cash income in the village; without it they would have great difficulty getting through the winter.

Sailing westward from Alaska Peninsula you would pass Unimak Island, the first of the Aleutian chain, separated from the mainland by narrow Isanotski Strait, or False Pass. This is the largest of the eastern Aleutians, and the home of magnificent Shishaldin Volcano, locally referred to as Smoking Moses. Several times in recent years Shishaldin, which rises majestically for almost ten thousand feet, has been in eruption. Faint wreaths of smoke and vapor still drift from its summit, making a striking picture, for the volcano is largely snow-clad. Pogromni Volcano, whose Russian name means "desolation," is a smaller conical peak near the western end of the island, also snow-covered.

Akutan Island, largest of the Krenitzin group, was once an important whaling station. Commercial whaling is no longer a local industry, but the Aleut settlement remains.

Unalaska, the next large island, is mountainous and during

*Unalaska
is the largest town
in the Aleutians.
Note Russian Orthodox
Church to which
the Aleuts still belong.*

the greater part of the year its higher elevations remain snowy. Makushin Volcano, more than six thousand feet high, forms the peak of the island. Unalaska Bay, on the northern shore and open to Bering Sea, is one of the most important bays in western Alaska. It contains the harbors of Iliuliuk Bay, Unalaska Harbor and Dutch Harbor.

The port of Unalaska, founded by Solovief in the eighteenth century as a fur trading station, was officially opened as a U.S. Customs port during the Klondike Gold Rush. It had been

much used by American and Russian vessels for years before that since it is a good halfway station for ships plying between Seattle and Nome. Food and fuel supplies were stored here for emergency uses. With the passing of the Gold Rush and the disappearance of bowhead whaling, which ceased around 1906, the village has declined.

Dutch Harbor in Unalaska Bay was once a flourishing settlement and the capital of the fur sealing industry. The United States Navy built a base here which in June, 1942, was the scene of the first Japanese attack upon North America.

Umnak Island, separated from Unalaska by Umnak Pass, is about seventy miles long and is the third largest island of the chain. It was once well populated but only a single village, Nikolski, survives today. Not far from Chaluka (the old Aleut name for the town) is a prospering sheep ranch with a flock of some three thousand. They produced fifteen thousand pounds of wool in 1957, which was flown out to Anchorage. Sheep ranching is not new on Umnak. The Russians brought the first stock to the island, recognizing ideal grazing in its rich meadows. In common with all the Aleutians, winter temperatures here are mild, keeping winter losses down to less than 15 per cent. Umnak sheep average three hundred pounds, live weight.

Atka Island, the largest of the Andreanof group, contains Korovin Volcano which rises about four thousand feet. Aleut women on Atka, and on Attu also, were famous for their exquisite baskets of beach grass which often took two or more years to complete. Wild rye, which commonly grows on Aleutian beaches to a height of four to five feet, was the grass used for making mats as well as baskets. It was gathered in the fall as it began to turn brown, split into thin strands and bleached. Then the long process of weaving began, with the grass kept moist and pliable by being wrapped in something damp. In recent times, bits of colored embroidery silk were woven with the grass to produce beautiful designs. The result was a watertight masterpiece, prized by Aleut and white man alike. Most of these baskets are now to be found only in museums or in the collections of a lucky few.

The rest of the Andreanof Islands are relatively unimportant, but they have strange, musical names like Koniuji, Igitkin, Kanaga, Tanaga, Kavalga, Unalga, Ulak, and Ilak.

Kiska, one of the Rat Islands, has more level ground than most of the islands, and the best harbor in the area. In World War II it was occupied for a time by the Japanese after the attack on Dutch Harbor.

At the end of the chain are the Near Islands, Agattu, and the outermost Attu, now completely deserted. Across the International Date Line, the Komandorski Islands, belonging to the Soviet Union, form a continuation of the Aleutian arc, reaching toward Kamchatka and another way of life.

Chapter Seven

Other Alaskan Cities

INTERNATIONAL HUB—ALASKA'S LARGEST

Anchorage is the largest city in Alaska. It contains magnificent new schools, attractive modern housing developments, excellent shops, luxurious hotels, more than one daily newspaper, and several radio and TV stations. Its expanding population, sixty thousand in 1958, is young, energetic, progressive, and optimistic.

Alaska's first International Airport in Anchorage points to a new role being played by the city as airlines, flying great circle routes across the Arctic Sea from Europe to Asia, stop here to refuel. In November, 1956, Scandinavian Airlines, a pioneer in northern flying, inaugurated the first route to fly directly across the geographic North Pole on its Copenhagen to Tokyo run. After flying northward across Scandinavia and Spitsbergen to the pinpoint called the Pole, the planes fly southward across the Beaufort Sea and Alaska to Anchorage where they refuel before continuing on to the Orient. The largest, most luxurious airplanes in the world now land here, and interesting people from the far corners of the world and local Anchorage folk may inspect each other at leisure. With pomp and ceremony the first SAS flight on this run included both Danish and Japanese royalty and great names from the newsman's world. Planes started from both Tokyo and Copenhagen and had a rendezvous at the Pole. Other airlines making trans-polar flights are following SAS's example, adding to Anchorage's increasing international renown.

Another event of interest to all Alaska occurred just outside Anchorage in the late summer of 1957. An oil strike was made by the Richfield Company which holds great promise for the entire population. The presence of oil in commercial quantities close by Alaska's largest city started an "oil rush" throughout the Kenai Peninsula. To date every drop of fuel oil burned in Alaska has had to be imported and the costly freight charges added to the retail price. This probably accounts for the excitement that swept the country and crowded other news off the front pages of all newspapers when word of "oil in our back yard" first reached Anchorage. True, the Navy some years before had drilled for oil and found it around Umiat and elsewhere in the Point Barrow region, but that had been in a Naval Reserve Area and held no meaning for the average citizen interested in keeping down the cost of his fuel bills.

Anchorage is the home of the largest native hospital in Alaska, as well as the Arctic Health Research Center, both vital factors in the newly successful war against tuberculosis and other diseases.

In 1940 the first detachment of United States troops arrived in Anchorage to start work on a new air base. Today the huge installations of Fort Richardson and Elmendorf Field have swelled both the temporary and permanent populations, and increased the prosperity of local business men. Anchorage is

Fourth Avenue in Anchorage.

only one spot, but a central, key one, in a tremendous network of airfields, bases, DEW Line, and White Alice Stations which make the defense industry Alaska's largest. The defense business employs more people over a wider area, spends more dollars, and brings in more outside workers and specialists than any other industry. Some of the men brought in to build or man these posts will stay on, to live out their lives in our new state.

THE GOLDEN HEART OF ALASKA

The word *gold* has a glamorous sound! It has power, too, enough to lure thousands of hopefuls to Alaska around the turn of this century, and it meant different things to different

Anchorage has the largest native hospital in Alaska.

people. Some who came wanted a fortune, overnight, if possible. Some were fleeing the crowded, dirty cities and wanted only untainted air to breathe and lots of space. Many were running from trouble, real or imagined—family, work, or money trouble. For some older men it was the last, lone hope of making a "success." A few women, considered very daring, came too. Idealists, cynics, workers, loafers, adventurers, and writers—they all poured into the territory. There was plenty of room for them in Alaska.

Some lucky few struck gold, but far more eventually gave up prospecting and turned to keeping shops, restaurants, and roadhouses. The fortunate ones who knew a trade like carpentering, found it more lucrative in the long run than panning gold. These "sourdoughs" formed the nucleus of many Alaskan towns, including Fairbanks.

In 1902 Felix Pedro discovered gold on what is now Pedro Creek. By September of the same year enough stampeders

had arrived to hold a meeting, appoint a recorder, and name the place "Fairbanks" after their vice-president.

News of the strike spread rapidly, but it was followed by disappointment when the gold-bearing bedrock was found to be buried eighty to a hundred feet under muck and gravel, much of it frozen hard in the permafrost. This meant that expensive equipment was needed to extract the gold. While it was hard on the lone prospector, it prevented the kind of mushroom development that nearly or quite wrecked several other Gold Rush towns.

In many sections around Fairbanks the rich pay dirt was worked out long ago. Nevertheless, for some years the largest and most productive gold mining operation in Alaska has been that of the U.S. Smelting, Mining and Refining Company outside Fairbanks. Mass production mining undertaken by million dollar corporations is the fashion now and while it has taken over the major portion of the industry, the small operator is still going strong. Giant gold dredges, resembling nothing so much as live dinosaur-like monsters, creak and groan at their work of taking bites out of the countryside, digesting the ore, retaining the precious parts, and spitting out the slag. They operate continuously, twenty-four hours a day. Although a relatively small crew operates the dredge and its accompanying gear, the machinery is most expensive, requiring enormous capital investment.

Gold mining is still an important economic factor around Fairbanks, but so too is transportation, logging, forestry, agriculture, tourism, higher education, and in recent years, defense.

A huge gold dredge operating near Fairbanks. Below are the tailings left behind when operations are completed.

141

Fairbanks is on the Tanana, a branch of the mighty Yukon River, about 120 miles south of the Arctic Circle. It is our farthest north, big, progressive city. Because it is an administrative, transportation, and supply center for the interior and entire north slope of Alaska, Fairbanks has a commercial importance beyond its size. Often called the "Golden Heart of Alaska," its trade area is estimated at 227,000 square miles. Both the Alaska Railroad and the Alaska Highway terminate at Fairbanks, which had about ten thousand inhabitants in 1958. The Tanana Valley is one of the best farming regions in Alaska, especially for cereals, but full advantage has not yet been taken of its agricultural possibilities.

The possible hours of sunshine in Fairbanks can vary from four hours in midwinter to nearly twenty-two in summer. Being far from the ocean and its climatic influences, Alaska's second largest city is generally both colder in winter and hotter in summer than coastal settlements. During the long summer days which darken only to a bright twilight around midnight, Fairbanks' temperatures frequently rise to 90° in the shade—the record is 99°F. In winter as nights grow longer the cold becomes intense. The thermometer drops to 60° below or lower (the record low is —66°F.) and the air becomes breathlessly still, for seldom do winds blow at extremely low temperatures, except in the Antarctic. While some activity stops, the railroad continues to run, bringing mail, freight, and passengers; planes arrive and take off—life goes on.

FARTHEST NORTH COLLEGE

Only five miles from Fairbanks at a town appropriately named College, is the farthest north institution of higher learning in North America, the University of Alaska. Its cluster of handsome modern buildings on the slope of College Hill is surrounded by one of the innumerable magnificent views in Alaska. The distant Alaska Range forms a cyclorama behind the buildings and on clear days students can see Mount Mc-Kinley from their classroom windows. Starting with a mere six students in 1922 when it was called the Alaska Agricultural College and School of Mines, by 1935 it had grown sufficiently in enrollment and quality to become a university. Thanks to the completion of new dormitory buildings in 1958 its enrollment may now reach nine hundred.

Dr. Charles Bunnell was the College's first president and served until 1949. He used to say, "Nobody is *sent* to college here," for he believed that a larger percentage of students worked their way through the University of Alaska than any comparable school in the more southerly states. There is no tuition fee for Alaskans, who make up between two-thirds to three-quarters of the student body. Students do much of the work on the campus, and in summer find jobs with nearby mining and construction companies. Much of the food consumed on the campus is supplied by one of the University's own agricultural experiment stations. The college offers a traditional liberal arts curriculum, but also special courses in mining and metallurgy, agriculture, engineering, geophysics, geology, and wildlife management.

The School of Mines is ideally located, for within a radius of twenty miles almost every kind of mining can be found in actual operation—lode, gold dredge, hydraulic, shovel dragline, and drift placer. Field trips to these sites speed learning, so that on graduation firsthand knowledge of every phase or type of mining operation has been gained. The campus has a complete mill for refining gold ores where students are trained to take part in professional operations. Ores submitted by prospectors and miners throughout the state are tested here.

The University of Alaska has a beautiful setting. It is the farthest north institution of higher learning in North America.

Although the average student is hard-working and serious, he misses none of the fun that is a part of all college life. Hockey, baseball, skiing, skating, wildlife study, and music groups, organized and unorganized, form an important segment of student life. A weekly student newspaper, *Polar Star*, is published, and a yearbook, *The Denali*. The college also publishes an official quarterly called *The Farthest North Collegian.*

Many interesting institutions, far from the Fairbanks area, are linked to the college. Under contract with the U. S. Navy's Office of Naval Research, the University operates the Point Barrow Arctic Research Laboratory. It works closely with the Frick Laboratories of the American Museum of Natural History in New York City to recover fossils of prehistoric animals from local dredging operations. In co-operation with the U. S. Coast and Geodetic Survey, it continuously records both the

Scientists at the Point Barrow Arctic Research Laboratory classifying plants.

*On the University campus a radio telescope is shown here silhouetted
against an auroral sky.*

earth's magnetism and seismographic tremors. More recently it has been tracking "sputniks" and other earth satellites.

An extraordinary number of scientists constantly streams in and out of the University, summer and winter, as northern science generally widens its boundaries. The college has become a logical center for many types of arctic research, especially since the erection of its Geophysical Institute. The latter now has a staff of eighty-six high-caliber scientists, many of them with worldwide reputations. The Institute played an important part in and was a data gathering center for the International Geophysical Year of 1957-58. It continues to broaden its extensive research program of studying the aurora, upper atmosphere phenomena, and numerous other aspects of geophysics.

A recent development which has multiplied the University's educational influence has been the establishment of affiliated community colleges at Anchorage, Juneau-Douglas, and Ketchikan, and Military Branch programs on the principal bases. Summer schools and a popular five-day Workshop on Alaska bring many Alaskans and non-Alaskans to the campus.

The University has a fine museum started as a result of Dr. Otto W. Geist's expeditions to St. Lawrence Island. A pioneer in Alaskan paleonthology, Dr. Geist has gathered a now famous collection of fossil materials to add to the historical items in the museum.

Strangely enough the gold mining companies have been the richest source of fossil skeleton remains of Alaska's prehistoric beasts. Dredging operations on nearby creeks in and around Fairbanks turned up quantities of bones from animals that roamed the country tens of thousands of years ago. It was Dr. Geist, a faculty member, who first realized that this was a "golden" opportunity in a non-metallic sense. He obtained the co-operation of the U. S. Smelting, Refining and Mining Company, the American Museum of Natural History, and the University, to permit him to rescue these important scientific finds. He educated the mining operators to send for him if any promising bit of ancient bone was revealed as they worked. Geist would then dash to the spot, excavate the site carefully, and only then would mining continue. Thanks to the perfect deepfreeze qualities of permafrost, centuries-dead mammoths, some with their flesh and hair still partly there, have been preserved.

Another area where students gain practical as well as theoretical knowledge at the University is in anthropology. Each summer field trips under college sponsorship are made to study both the Eskimos and the other Indians, often with a professor acting as leader. Archeological work is sometimes done at the same time or on separate expeditions.

A startling archeological find was made in Alaska in 1939 and 1940 by two faculty members, Froelich G. Rainey and Louis Giddings, and by a visiting Danish Eskimo archeologist, Helge Larsen. At Point Hope, a peninsula in northwestern Alaska which juts into the Polar Sea, they discovered the remains of a unique arctic metropolis. They unearthed a group of eight hundred dwellings arranged in regular avenues which must have housed a population larger than that of prewar Fairbanks! Point Hope is 130 miles north of the Arctic Circle, beyond 68° north latitude.

The site, called Ipiutak, is thought to have been built well over a thousand years ago. Excavations yielded beautiful ivory carvings, some of them unlike those of any known northern Eskimo or Indian culture. About five hundred skeletons were recovered. In strange tombs, fashioned of logs, skeletons were revealed which stared up at the archeologists with artificial eyeballs carved of ivory and inlaid with huge jet pupils. Before burial the natural eyes had apparently been gouged

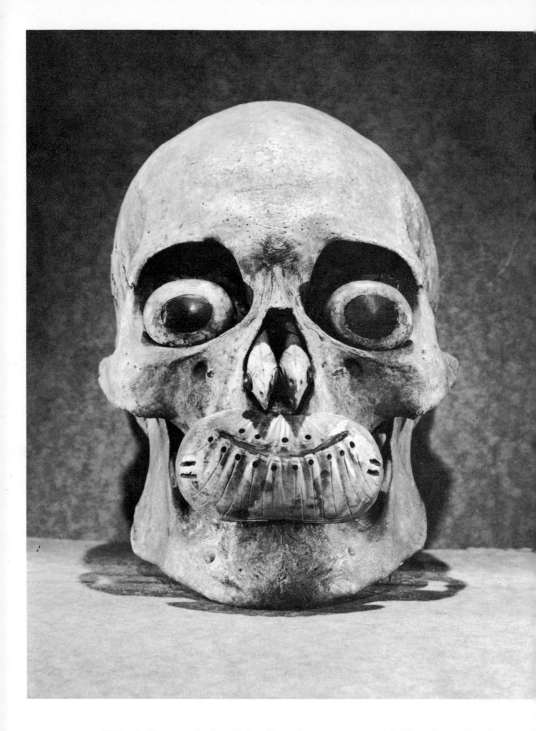

This skull unearthed at Point Hope has ivory eyes inlaid with pupils of jet, and ivory nose plug and mouth cover.

out and replaced with ivory substitutes. Ivory mouth covers and nose plugs carved to represent bird beaks added to the fantastic appearance of the skulls. Exquisite spiral carvings of walrus ivory, of unknown use, and delicately made and engraved implements were found in the burials. Many designs of the artifacts resembled those produced in North China two or three thousand years ago, others were like carvings of the Ainu peoples in northern Japan and the Amur River natives of Siberia. This was not the culture of a simple people, but a highly sophisticated, complex group.

Twentieth century Point Hope, or *Tigerak*, "the forefinger," as it is known to the Eskimos, supports a flourishing population of about three hundred. The question arises as to how such a large settlement as nearby Ipiutak could have been fed. The answer that comes quickly to mind is the location of Point Hope, directly in the path of the annual northward migration of the bowhead whale. But archeological evidence tells us that Ipiutak folk did no whaling but lived rather on walrus, hair seal, and the huge 900-pound *ugrug*, or bearded seal. If they did no whaling, their direct descendents do. Indeed, their lives center around the pursuit of the mightiest mammal in the Arctic.

MATANUSKA—AGRICULTURAL EXPERIMENT

The University of Alaska maintains one of several agricultural experiment stations near Matanuska. Six miles to the northeast, on a branch of the Alaska Railroad, is the "Matanuska Colony" at the town of Palmer. This is the working center of the Alaska Rural Rehabilitation Corporation which during the depression years transported more than two hundred families to Alaska to start a new life. Between March and June of 1935, 903 colonists chosen from the relief roles of

*A farm
in Matanuska Valley.
The University
maintains an
agricultural experiment
station near Matanuska.*

northern Minnesota, Wisconsin, and Michigan arrived at Palmer. Later they were joined by people from other localities. They lived in tents until the land was cleared and houses built. Money for equipment, purchase of land, buildings, livestock, and furniture was lent by the Federal Government. By the fall of 1936 the farmers' newly built barns were bulging with harvested crops and Palmer was growing into a flourishing town.

As often happens in a large, planned government project, there were some discontented people with no talent for or interest in farming, who deserted the colony. The newspapers featured their stories, leaving many with the impression that the experiment had been a failure. A certain amount of unnecessary regimentation, and much poor planning, largely due to Washington's lack of information, hampered the early years of the colony. But no one who has seen the flourishing town of Palmer recently, and the rich farms that surround it, would connect the word "failure" with the area. For in addition to its beauty, this is a fertile, prospering valley with an aura of success. The new supermarket, the huge drugstore which is really a department store (for it sells food, books, camera equipment, hardware, and toys in addition to drugs), the restaurants, beauty shops—all testify to a healthy self-supporting community.

The increased demand for fresh milk, cream, and vegetables, plus Palmer's excellent road, rail, and air connections, seems to assure a prosperous future. The Matanuska Valley already grows more than half of all the farm products raised in Alaska. Milk, potato, poultry and egg production, in that order, are the most important crops. As Fairbanks is the market for most of the Tanana Valley farming, so Anchorage, fifty miles away, is Palmer's chief consumer.

The Glenn Highway connects Palmer with the Richardson Highway, which in turn connects with the Alaska Highway and

Fairbanks. "Matanuska Maid" products are shipped by truck, rail, ship, and air to as far away as the Canadian Pacific Coast and Fairbanks. Nearby Eklutna is the scene of an important water power project which supplies ample power to Palmer as well as the entire Anchorage area.

The farmers' co-operative at Palmer is said to have handled six million dollars' worth of produce in 1957. At the close of each growing season an Agricultural Fair draws visitors locally as well as from far places. Palmer's setting, between two dramatic glacier-studded mountain ranges, the Talkeetnas and the Chugachs, makes it a delightful goal for pleasure trips. At the 1958 Fair a sixty-pound cabbage grown by Max Sherrod broke what is believed to be the world's record for size and weight. On the Sherrod farm his wife showed me a sunflower reaching above the second story roof of their farmhouse! It is commonplace to see sweetpeas in Palmer, and throughout southeastern and south central Alaska, ten feet tall, with enormous, brilliant blossoms. Every familiar flower seems taller, bigger-blossomed, and brighter-colored than those we are accustomed to in more southerly latitudes.

FISH IS STILL KING

Long before the coming of the white man Alaska's salmon provided the prime source of food for Indians living on the coast and inland along rivers. In 1878 the first commercial canneries were established and within the fifty-year period following, according to Ernest Gruening, Alaska had become the world's greatest salmon producer. Salmon surpassed gold mining as her major industry; salmon represented the largest capital investment, showed the biggest annual financial yield, and the industry was the greatest employer of labor.

Salmon became "the largest single source of territorial revenue, and the dominant factor in Alaska's political, economic, and social life."

In recent years the size of the annual salmon runs has declined sharply. Some say over fishing is the cause, others blame insufficient or poorly enforced conservation measures; a few experts say the reason is still unknown. The shallow arm of Bristol Bay, formerly one of the richest salmon fishing areas

in the world has declined so rapidly that some consider it should be closed for an indefinite period to give the runs a chance to revive. Nevertheless the 1957 salmon catch alone was valued at seventy-nine million dollars. During late summer and fall millions of salmon still swim in Alaskan waters on their way to spawn.

That every fish seeks unerringly the river and branch stream of its birth and early development seems so romantic a

An Indian fish camp on the Tanana River.

notion that many have doubted it. Alaskan salmon are known to travel thousands of miles from home, spending the major part of their lives, in the world's largest ocean, the Pacific.

Salmon are hatched in fresh water where they remain two years and then descend to the sea. When they migrate outbound they are only a few inches long. They grow rapidly in salt water and two or three years later, fully grown, they return, "each to the stream where it was born," to spawn and die. It is on this homeward migration that the fish are taken for commercial purposes.

A closeup of the Indian fish camp on the Tanana River.

Next to Bristol Bay, Ketchikan is probably the most important fishing center in Alaska. It is often called the Salmon Canning Capital of the World. Through islands of green forest, gliding along mirror-still waters, a ship rounds another bend and comes upon Ketchikan, the southernmost good-sized city in Alaska.

Robert Ellis, a leading citizen of Ketchikan, has described the city as being "three blocks wide and three miles long." Strung out thinly along a narrow strip of land at the foot of sharply rising Deer Mountain, it seems in imminent danger of tumbling into the waters of Tongass Narrows. Every square inch of the crowded city has been utilized and when new streets are needed it is said that they must be blasted out of the solid rock. Only pontoon planes arrive at Ketchikan, for there is no airfield in town and no room to build one. All but the small sea planes land across the water at Annette Island.

A giant new pulp mill, one of the largest in the world, was recently completed in Ketchikan, increasing the town's population considerably. It is a brand new year-round industry for Alaska and employs a thousand people, half in town and half in the woods. Timber for the mill is cut from the Tongass National Forest's sixteen million acres of virgin timber which occupy most of southeastern Alaska. All cutting is under the strict supervision of the United States Forest Service. Other pulp mills are planned for Alaska; one at Sitka is nearing completion and Juneau and Wrangell are being discussed as potential sites.

Ketchikan has skyscraper apartment buildings, modern schools, and attractive new housing developments. The ten-thousand or so people who live here enjoy the cool summers which resemble those of the Maine coast. There is little snowfall in winter, but in all seasons there is rain, rain, and more rain. The abundant rainfall is responsible for ideal tree grow-

Ketchikan is strung out along a narrow strip of land at the foot of Deer Mountain. Note fishing boats in harbor.

A pulp mill at Ketchikan.

ing conditions in the area and also for the famous Ketchikan flower gardens. Delphiniums reach eight or nine feet, pansies grow as big as saucers, anything that grows does so lushly here. The harbor is a colorful sight too, crowded with innumerable fishing boats bringing their catches in to be canned or frozen and shipped out. Although no road connects Ketchikan with other towns, the streets are crowded with automobiles. The city is in touch with the rest of Alaska and "outside," through shipping, and numerous daily flights radiating in several directions.

ALASKA'S FARTHEST NORTH

A glance at a polar projection map of the Northern Hemisphere, or better, at the top of a globe, shows the countries of the North grouped around a smallish sea formerly called the Arctic Ocean, but now usually the Arctic Sea or, more descriptively, the Polar Mediterranean. As the Old World Mediterranean lies between Europe and Africa, so our northernmost body of water, surrounded by the powerful nations of the world, lies between North America in the shape of Greenland, Canada, and Alaska on one side, and northern Europe and Asia on the other.

On the shores of the Polar Mediterranean the most northerly cape in our most northerly state is Point Barrow. As the planes fly it is five hundred miles northeast of Nome and the same distance northwest of Fairbanks. Its Eskimo name is *Nuwuk*, meaning "the point." Our name for it dates from 1826 when Captain Beechey named it after Sir John Barrow, the great British patron of arctic exploration who was responsible for Parliament's offering a twenty thousand pound reward to the first navigator sailing the Northwest Passage.

About nine miles southwest of Point Barrow is the village of Barrow. It was here that a trading post was first established in 1885 by the later famous Charles D. Brower. The post is still flourishing, although Charles is gone now and his son Tom runs it. Charlie Brower played host to many famous explorers in the more than fifty years he lived in Barrow. Will Rogers and Wiley Post were on their way to visit him when their plane crashed and both lost their lives. In his book, *Fifty Years Below Zero*, Brower gives the highlights of his long and interesting life. Tom Brower continues the family tradition as an unofficial greeter and influential citizen. He sells

Eskimo children at Point Barrow.

canned milk at cost in his store, and makes his profit on luxury items. Tom is prosperous these days.

But nowadays a great many more people turn up at Barrow than ever did in his father's day. There is a DEW Line Station here. The Office of Naval Research has a growing Arctic Research Laboratory, staffed by permanent scientists and visited every summer by others. Here from well-equipped and -staffed modern laboratories they investigate a tremendous range of subjects, from the physiological adaptations of man and animals to cold, to the physics of the offshore sea ice. Big ships may be seen anchored offshore at Barrow, and military installations in the area swell the population.

An innovation of recent years is the tourist business. In summer regular flights are scheduled several times weekly, and bring vacationers from many parts of the continent to Barrow. People come who want to set foot on the northernmost

tip of Alaska, see how the Eskimos live, and perhaps ↑
ride in a skin-covered umiak. For Barrow Eskimos, al↑
most of them have had high wages working on defense installations, still hunt walrus and whale as their ancestors did.
There is now a Top of the World Hotel at Point Barrow, owned
and operated by Eskimos, to accommodate the visitors. If the
weather is nippy, and it often is here even in summer, fur-
trimmed parkas are supplied by the airline hostess.

Further tourist entertainment is provided of a summer eve-
ning at the Eskimo Dance House. Here to the accompaniment
of high-pitched singing and the hypnotic sound of a dozen
drums beating complicated rhythms in perfect unison, Eskimo
dances are performed in full costume. While tourists make up

Drum dance at Barrow. Eskimos formerly had no word of greeting. Now
koyanuk, *which means excellent, is used in many areas.*

the larger part of the audience, they are joined by many middle-aged and older local residents who still love to hear the old songs, and see the traditional dances. The younger set seems to prefer rock-and-roll dancing down the street a bit, to the strains of a gaudy juke box. The flared skirts of the young girls swirl and twist as they expertly perform their complicated steps. At a distance they look like any group of teen-agers performing the same ritual in more southerly places.

Barrow is in truly arctic country. More than three hundred miles north of the Arctic Circle, it is far from any warm currents like those of the Gulf Stream that bathe the northern coasts of Norway in similar latitudes. Here great masses of ice, pressed forward by wind and current, grind against the shore in winter, producing the heaviest ice pack known in any part of the world. There is permafrost here; only from about six to eighteen inches of the earth's surface thaws downward in summer. Because of the permafrost below, the hot sun above, and the absence of sidewalks, the streets are muddy, and boots, whether rubber or sealskin, are a must. The frost below the surface which creates so many building problems, happily provides free refrigeration for the food storage chambers dug into frozen soil. Meat has been kept fresh for years in these natural deepfreezes. Where the vegetation is undisturbed, the meadows are covered with rich grass.

As in all other towns in the permafrost zone of Alaska, water for drinking, cooking, and bathing presents a problem. In Point Barrow and similar towns, water must be hauled, often from great distances, and is sold by the drum. This makes bathing as we know it an expensive luxury, for each barrel of water costs $1.50. If the family is large there is no question of a daily bath. Water for laundry and cleaning purposes must also be purchased, increasing the already fearfully high cost of living. But if the cost of living is high, so are wages, and on the whole the Barrow people think of themselves as prospering mightily.

Though the streets may be muddy in summer, the attractive English-speaking Eskimo girls, wearing jewel-colored velvet parkas trimmed with becoming white fox or wolverine, may be seen strolling along in pairs and groups. The latest style harlequin-shaped eye glasses will be worn with a coat the design of which is centuries old, although its material is purchased at the store, and it may have a zipper added.

The farthest tip of our northernmost sandspit is not the boundary marking the end of all activity. Yankee whalers learned a century ago that fortunes could be built in Massachusetts on whalebone from the sea beyond the coast. Stefansson proved on his 1913-18 sledge journeys over the ice that life in the sea does not cease beyond where ships are able to penetrate. His parties lived by hunting seals as they traveled afoot over the moving pack ice many hundreds of miles north of Alaskan land. Later Papanin and his colleagues demonstrated, in 1937, that the waters of the Polar Mediterranean are teeming with animal and plant life even at the very North Pole, more than a thousand miles north of Barrow. Recently there have been many scientific stations set down on the polar pack, both by the Soviets and by us.

In August of 1958 the nuclear-powered submarine *Nautilus* completed a passage under the pack ice, from Bering Strait to the North Pole, emerging in the Greeland Sea north of Iceland. Her sister ship the *Skate* soon afterward made the same magnificent journey in the opposite direction, surfacing at the North Pole itself, and three hundred miles on the Alaska side of it, to greet and visit with the scientists on the drifting sea ice station Alpha, engaged in International Geophysical Year investigations.

In the Arctic the North Pole is the center of a deep, liquid sea. This is exactly opposite to the Antarctic, where a huge ice-covered continent surrounds the South Pole. A surprising number of people still hold the erroneous belief, which dates back to classic Greek times, that the Arctic Sea is frozen to the bottom. Another misconception was encouraged by almost every newspaper and magazine reporting the *Nautilus* voyage, stating that the submarine traveled below the "icecap under the North Pole." There is no icecap at, under, or anywhere near the North Pole. By definition, an icecap is a large, land-based

The USS Nautilus *welcomed home to Groton. PANOPOS (on signs) stands for "Pacific Atlantic North Pole".*

The USS Skate *is nearly obscured by ice as she surfaces near the North Pole.*

glacier composed of fresh ice, which in earlier times was newly fallen snow. The relatively thin, fractured shell of ice which floats on our northernmost sea, is salt water ice, which has a different composition, freezing point, color, texture and behaviour under pressure or melting, than fresh ice. Sea ice may range in thickness from fractions of an inch to a maximum thickness of eleven to thirteen feet.

Arctic Sea ice would resemble a thin, smooth shell, were it not for winds and currents. Winds, however gentle, and currents, however sluggish, are sufficient to break the cover into ice floes of every imaginable shape and size and to keep them constantly on the move. In winter they move rather slowly; in summer they move somewhat more freely, the spaces between floes widening to reveal more patches of blue, open water. In midsummer as much as 25 per cent of the Polar Sea may be open water where whales and submarines alike may surface with ease.

Winds and currents which break the ice cover are also responsible for grinding the floes against each other at their edges, or piling them up into pressure ridges against the landfast shore ice, where it meets the moving pack. These pressure ridges, startling and dramatic in size and shape, are seldom higher above water than one hundred feet. Two hundred feet therefore is about the maximum thickness of sea ice above and below water. For a pressure ridge, if you visualize the whole of it, is usually pyramid-shaped, the base of the pyramid below water level.

Another misconception about the Arctic Sea is that it is filled with innumerable icebergs. Practically speaking, there are no icebergs in the Arctic Sea. Greenland, our greatest northern iceberg factory, discharges its bergs to the east and west, but all are borne southward by the prevailing currents and eventually they die in the warm waters of the North Atlantic. All icebergs were once part of a glacier and their ice is therefore fresh. When a glacier extends down to the sea, and out over the water, it is the floating section that breaks off to become an iceberg, and the birth process is called *calving*.

To further complicate the differences between salt and fresh ice, salt sea ice when it is sufficiently old, becomes fresh. In alternate freezing and thawing that occurs with the changing season, the salt content of sea ice migrates toward whichever side is warmer, usually downward, and the briny particles are eventually eliminated. When sea ice is more than two years old its melt water can be used for drinking. After three years, no saltiness in floating sea ice can be detected except by delicate chemical test—the human palate cannot detect it. This has been known for centuries by the practical sealers and whalers who wintered often in the North.

As we chart the drifts in the Arctic Sea, investigate the underwater mountains, life in the ocean, the structure of the ice, the weather above it, and the upper atmosphere, new words become part of our language and there is a new and valuable understanding of scientific problems. As a network of air routes makes a kind of Times Square of the North Pole, and navigators aboard luxury planes exchange information with scientists on the ice below, we enter a new era where man may roam at will anywhere in the world, even below the pack ice, and perhaps soon to outer space. There are no longer any "remote places" on the globe.

✂ *Index* ✂

Index

Index

Index

Kodiak Island, 35, 36
Komandorski Islands, 125, 135
Koniuji Island, 135
Krenitzin Islands, 132
Kuskokwin River, 49, 83, 120

Larsen, Helge, 149
Larsson, Ernest B., 90
Laughlin, William, 125
Little Diomede Island, 107-111
Londborg, Maynard D., 84

Machetanz, Fred and Sara, 104-106
Matanuska, 151-155
Matanuska Maid products, 155
Matanuska Valley, 29-30
Mekoryuk, 122
Mendenhall Glacier, 44
Mining, 29; gold, 138-141
Mosquitoes, 15-16
Mt. Edgecumbe, 36, 38
Mt. Edgecumbe Boarding School, 38, 85
Mt. Juneau, 40
Mt. McKinley, 9, 19, 143
Mt. McKinley National Park, 19-20
Mt. Roberts, 40
Musk oxen, 117-119
Muskeg, 21

National Wildlife Refuge, Nunivak Island, 117
Native Arts and Crafts Service, 122
Nautilus submarine voyage, 167, 168
Near Islands, 123, 131, 135
New Archangel, 36
Nikolski (Chaluka), 126, 134
Noatak River, 49
Nome, 81, 120, 134, 163
North Pole, 19, 21, 136, 137, 167-168
Northern Consolidated Airlines, 79
Northwest Passage, 163
Norton Sound, 81
Nunivak Island, 116-123; Eskimos, 116-117, 120-123

Oil, 8, 29, 137

Paleontology, University of Alaska, 148-149
Palmer, 154-155
Papanin, Ivan, 167
Pedro Creek, 139
Pedro, Felix, 139

Permafrost, 16, 141, 149, 166
Peter the Great, 109
Petropavlovsk, 128
Point Barrow, 3, 13, 18, 33, 88, 117, 163-167; Naval Oil Reserve Area near, 137
Point Barrow Arctic Research Laboratory, 79, 146
Point Hope, 33, 83, 149-151
Polar Mediterranean. SEE *Arctic Sea*
Population, 8, 9; Aleut, 125-126; Eskimo, 49; Little Diomede Island, 111
Post, Wiley, 163
Potlatch, 47-48
Pribilof, Gavriil, 112-113
Pribilof (Seal) Islands, 112-115, 131
Promyshlenniki, 126
Pulp. SEE *Timber and pulp industry*
Pulp mills, 29, 159

Railroads, 19
Rainey, Froelich G., 149
Rat Islands, 123, 128, 135
Reindeer herds, 96, Nunivak 119-122, Roundup, 120
Religion, 37, 82-84, 122, 128-130, 131
Richardson Highway, 154
Richfield Company, 137
Rivers, Ralph J., 4
Roads, 20-21
Rogers, Will, 163
Russian America, 34-38, 128-130
Russian American Company, 49
Russian (Greek) Orthodox Church, 37, 128-130. SEE ALSO *Religion*
Russians, 128-130, 134
Ryan, Frank, 92

St. George Island, 112-113
St. Lawrence Island, 148
St. Matthew Island, 120
St. Paul Island, 112, 113
Salmon, 28, 125
Salmon industry, 155-159
Saxman Park, 48
Scandinavian Airlines, 136-137
Schooling. SEE *Education*
Scurvy, 126-128
Sea lion, 115, 125
Sea otter, 126-128
Seal, bearded, 151
Seal Islands, SEE *Pribilof Islands*
Seal oil, 111